Backstage at *The Lost Colony*

Dwayne Walls Jr
DWAYNE WALLS JR.

COQUINA
PRESS

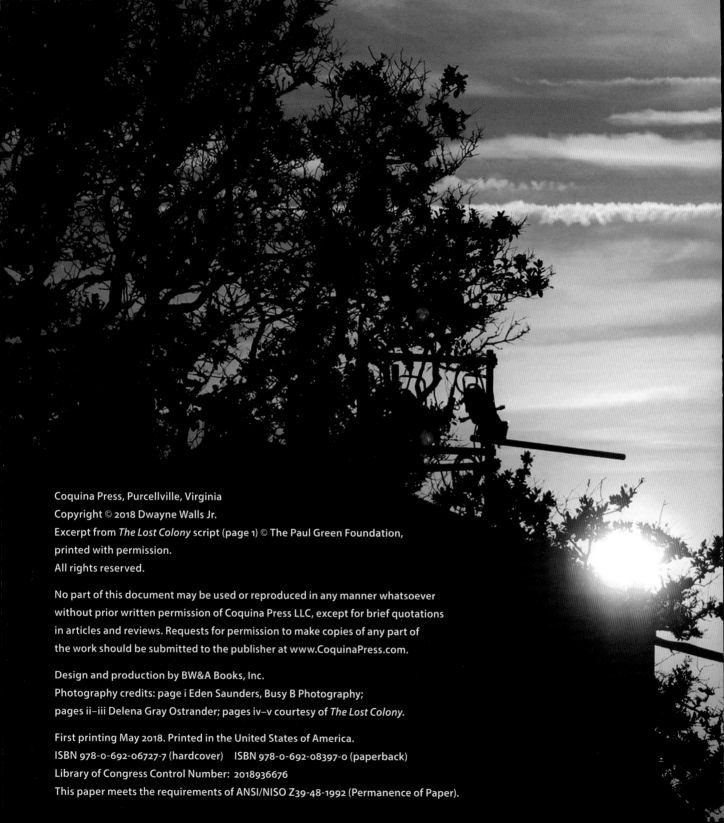

Coquina Press, Purcellville, Virginia
Copyright © 2018 Dwayne Walls Jr.
Excerpt from *The Lost Colony* script (page 1) © The Paul Green Foundation,
printed with permission.
All rights reserved.

Design and production by BW&A Books, Inc.
Photography credits: page i Eden Saunders, Busy B Photography;
pages ii–iii Delena Gray Ostrander; pages iv–v courtesy of *The Lost Colony*.

First printing May 2018. Printed in the United States of America.
ISBN 978-0-692-06727-7 (hardcover)   ISBN 978-0-692-08397-0 (paperback)
Library of Congress Control Number: 2018936676
This paper meets the requirements of ANSI/NISO Z39-48-1992 (Permanence of Paper).

CONTENTS

Photo by J. Aaron Trotman

FOREWORD

*F*or eight decades, *The Lost Colony* has defied the odds. From its improbable founding during the Great Depression through flood and fires, Paul Green's first and most famous symphonic outdoor drama is a study in resilience. And like the "lost" colonists of Roanoke Island who inspired the show, the people who created and sustained it and who continue to preserve its legacy are a study in passion and determination.

My fascination with *The Lost Colony* began in 1989. I had been hired the previous autumn by then–executive director Scott Parker to promote the show—a show I had never seen. At first, it was just a job, albeit a fun one, especially after I was joined in the public relations office by Elizabeth Evans, who had danced in the show in college. For months leading up to rehearsals, Elizabeth and I worked together in the relative quiet of *The Lost Colony* Building alongside about eight other year-round staff, including legends Bob Knowles, the curmudgeonly and beloved general manager, and Mabel Basnight, who ran—or rather ruled—the box office for more than fifty years.

Then, one day in May, the doors to our quiet building blew open to admit some 125 actors, singers, dancers, and technicians—mostly college students. They lit up Fort Raleigh National Historic Site with their luminous youth and their excitement over the promise of a summer honing their craft on the Outer Banks of North Carolina. Elizabeth and I grew accustomed to working to the strains of Elizabethan folk songs and Indian chants coming from the rehearsal hall just outside the office we shared.

Watching director Fred Chappell channel all that creative energy was a revelation to me. With every passing day, Fred and his artistic staff knit together the pieces of the show, until finally Paul Green's symphonic drama burst to life on Waterside Theatre's massive stage in front of a standing-room-only audience of Dare County residents. I had never seen anything like it. I was hooked.

Photo by Delena Gray Ostrander

Even after the cast and crew settled into the routine of six weekly performances, I spent many an evening backstage enjoying the easy camaraderie, the occasional antics, and the awe-inspiring sunsets. By summer's end, I was in love—with *The Lost Colony*, with Manteo, with Roanoke Island. Long after I moved on to other work and other worlds, my love for *The Lost Colony* remained. If anything, I feel ever more tightly tethered to my *Colony* experience and the *Colony* people, an extraordinary number of whom have gone on to live their dreams of careers in the performing arts.

I have long wanted to produce a book about life backstage at *The Lost Colony*. I imagined a collection of stories from alumni and present-day cast and crew, and when I broached the idea with Elizabeth Evans, her enthusiasm convinced me it had merit. After several months of chasing stories, however, it became apparent the book needed something more—a unifying narrative.

Right around that time, there appeared in my mailbox an essay by Dwayne Walls, whom I vaguely remembered from the 1990 season. The essay, part of which is included in the chapter "Yellow Stricken Sands," revealed Dwayne's natural gift for storytelling. Before long, we agreed that he would follow the cast and crew through *The Lost Colony*'s eightieth anniversary season, from rehearsals through strike.

I encouraged Dwayne to write not as a dispassionate observer but as someone whose own life and livelihood have been shaped in profound ways through his experience with *The Lost Colony*. I appreciated his equal affinity for noted producers, directors, and actors and for the men and women whose grinding toil is visible to the audience only in the form of exquisitely cared-for costumes, meticulously maintained sets and props, and scenery moved quickly on a darkened stage to the exact right spot.

In *Backstage at* The Lost Colony, our intent is not to offer a historical account of the show, although the book briefly discusses the drama's founding, important milestones, and near-death experiences. Rather, we want to offer readers a fresh look at a legend in American theater because, while we honor the past, we hope to illustrate that *The Lost Colony*, with its themes of freedom, community, hope, and optimism, is as relevant today as it was in 1937, when it premiered to a standing-room-only audience of more than two thousand.

There's a healthy tension between honoring the past and carrying a legacy forward. The challenge for today's artistic staff is to preserve the integrity of Paul Green's script while finding fresh ways to bring the story alive for modern audiences conditioned to amusements on small mobile screens. If the eightieth anniversary season is any indication, *The Lost Colony* in 2017, directed by Ira David Wood III, continued to defy the odds with a marked increase in attendance over recent years.

Maybe that's because *The Lost Colony* is all about dreams: the dreams of the colonists lost to history; the dreams of the show's creators, who never imagined their community drama would run for eighty years and counting; and the big dreams brought to Waterside Theatre's big stage by cast and crew members past and present.

This book is a love letter to them all.

——BARBARA LEARY, Editor and Publisher

PREFACE

*I*n 1983, when I was a nineteen-year-old theater major in college, I signed a $110-a-week contract to be an actor technician for *The Lost Colony*. Painfully provincial and dreadfully serious, I was enraged at a world that for some unfathomable reason refused to acknowledge me as the artistic genius I considered myself to be. I was also a starving artist; once the show opened, after taxes and a rent deduction for company housing in the Morrison Grove apartments, my weekly paycheck amounted to $67.69. I was broke and hungry, as indignant as a freshly shorn sheep and just as powerless. The beard I was required to grow for my part as a colonist came in so poorly that people thought I had dirt on my face, and it never stopped itching. I was the lowest of the low: I was a first-year AT.

But I was not alone. Other first-year guys were on the crew, and we gravitated toward each other, knowing instinctively that the only way we would survive the summer was by sticking together. I do not know who first called us "Space Puppies." I think it was another AT, but it could have been anyone. That's how we became known. Space Puppies missed cues. Space Puppies left their banners out in the rain. Space Puppies forgot to put their plumes in their helmets. Space Puppies forgot to return their props. Space Puppies got fined left and right because we screwed up everything we touched.

According to the master carpenter who ran the crew, we were the worst bunch of ATs who ever existed. When we screwed something up, either in the show or on a work call, the next day he would stand us in a line and bawl us out, cursing us in the vilest terms. We stood there and took it because we were just Space Puppies.

I did not have a good summer.

When it was over, I tried to forget the whole thing. By the time my intent-to-return letter arrived early the next year, I was a full-fledged 1980s New

Wave nightmare with a motorcycle, an asymmetrical haircut, stone-washed jeans, and a shiny new earring dangling from one lobe. I threw the letter away and swore I'd never grow a beard again.

But in May 1987, I needed a gig. I called *The Lost Colony*'s administrative offices, and a week later I was headed for Roanoke Island as a last-minute replacement for someone who'd backed out. I was twenty-three that season, no longer an angry or a hungry young artist, having graduated to being a struggling young artist. I had a great summer, even though my beard still itched. I had such a good time, in fact, that I came back and did it again in 1990. That summer, I considered myself an established artist, since by this time I had worked in regional theater and toured with a professional children's theater company.

I was sure *The Lost Colony* was a closed chapter of my life until seven years later, in 1997, when my buddy Hank Hale began his second year as technical director. Long before rehearsals started, Hank called me from New York and asked me to come to Manteo for a couple of weeks in May to work on the theater. The deck boards on the Queen's Stage were rotten and would have to be replaced to accept the weight of the new Queen's Chamber unit, which was arriving on trucks from a big shop in New York, to be assembled in place. I made him promise to cut me loose before the first company meeting.

We were a crew of about half a dozen and had a grand old time. The work was hard, but the weather was good, and there were porpoises off the back dock. We bunked in the "Beehive," one of those now-demolished cottages reserved for *Lost Colony* company members, and our nights were filled with laughter.

The laughter stopped when the Queen's Chamber trucks pulled into the parking lot; that's when I realized why Hank wanted me there. The set was opera house huge and opera house heavy and would require all of us to assemble it in place. Doing the job right took more than an extra week, so I stayed. Then I stayed longer and built wigwams; then I stayed even longer and built props. Before I knew it, the show was open and I was under contract as the properties master.

In 1998, I returned as the master carpenter and ran the AT crew, who put the place back together after Waterside Theatre underwent a renovation that included new seats and new proscenium walls. Looking back on my years in the show, I am proudest of the work that 1998 company accomplished, although weighing the differences between individual seasons makes for bad comparisons, since each company faces its own unique set of obstacles. Maybe I just love that crew the most.

If anyone had told me in 1983 that I would be part of more than 350 performances of *The Lost Colony* spread over fifteen years, I would have laughed in their face, yet I ended up living five sweet summers on Roanoke Island, each one as revelatory as a first kiss, and just as unforgettable. Those years doing the show were as rewarding as they were demanding, simultaneously artistically inspiring and physically exhausting. I reflect on my time with the show with intense satisfaction, and I hold the many friends I made in awesome regard.

The show turned eighty years old in 2017, a milestone in any lifetime, so I thought the best way to tell the story of being backstage at *The Lost Colony* would be to go to Roanoke Island and tell the story of the 2017 cast and crew. This is their *Lost Colony*. I was lucky enough to see it.

ONE

Honoring the Birthplace of a Nation

For here once walked the men of dreams,
The sons of hope and pain and wonder,
Upon their foreheads truth's bright diadem,
The light of the sun in their countenance,
And their lips singing a new song –
A song for ages yet unborn,
For us the children that came after them –
"O new and mighty world to be!"
They sang,
"O land majestic, free, unbounded!"

    This was the vision, this the fadeless dream –
    Tread softly, softly now these yellow stricken sands.
    This was the grail, the living light that leapt –
    Speak gently, gently on these muted tongueless shores.

Now down the trackless hollow years
That swallowed them but not their song
We send response –
"O lusty singer dreamer, pioneer,
Lord of the wilderness, the unafraid,
Tamer of darkness, fire and flood,
Of the soaring spirit winged aloft
On the plumes of agony and death –
Hear us, O hear!
The dream still lives,
It lives, it lives,
And shall not die!"

—Paul Green
Excerpt from 1937 Souvenir Program of John Borden's final speech.
Copyright Paul Green Foundation. Reprinted by permission.

Photo by Delena Gray Ostrander

A Return to Yellow Stricken Sands

The Lost Colony gave me lifelong respect for anyone performing in bare feet.

ON A CHILLY GRAY EVENING in the middle of May, after an absence of almost twenty years, I am backstage at Waterside Theatre on Roanoke Island, home of *The Lost Colony*. From the wing near the carpentry shop, looking onstage, I see actors rehearsing in the sand covering the stage.

I vividly remember the sand. Not the hot, white, sun-bleached sand that burned my toes and squeaked under my feet on Sundays—our days off—at Coquina Beach, but the show sand, the sand that followed me everywhere and lived in my hair and in my sheets and in every corner of my room; the sand I had with every meal; the dry sand I poured out of my shoes every chance I had to sit down; the wet sand that hit my face in clumps during scene shifts; the damp, sweat-soaked sand that at first I didn't dare and later didn't bother to brush off my skin because that only made it worse. Sand, sand everywhere, and it all had to be sifted, sifted by hand. As an actor technician, sifting the sand was just part of my job.

We found scary things in those big sieves during sand sifts, things we called "dancer traps." We uncovered nails, staples, and tacks from the scenery; sharp chunks of wood from the decking; safety pins, buttons, and snaps from costumes; even coins and jewelry. We found small animals that had been trampled to death during the show. Mice received a brief Christian burial while we sang the Final March hymn. Reptiles unceremoniously went into the sound.

One night in 1987, I was backstage when the dancers carried Mark Fields, the dancer playing Uppowoc, offstage early after the Indian Dance. He collapsed in the wing with a bloody six-inch shard of decking sticking from the bottom of his foot. Although in agony, he had managed to finesse the choreography and finish the dance. The memory came shrieking back to me eleven

Waterside Theatre's expansive stage is covered in sand, which must be sifted by hand every week, a task that falls to the actor technicians. Photo by Ira David Wood III

years later when Chris Graham, our Uppowoc of 1998, suffered the same injury in the same way during a preshow rehearsal.

As master carpenter, I called an emergency sand sift. I had everyone on their hands and knees scratching around like cats in a litter box, feeling and looking for anything that could hurt a foot. *The Lost Colony* gave me lifelong respect for anyone performing in bare feet.

Everyone onstage tonight is wearing shoes, since they are still early in rehearsals. The sun is sinking lower by the minute, and a steady wind blows out of the northwest, making the sixty-degree air feel colder than it is. A thin strip of clear sky to the west means a beautiful sunset tonight for this, my first sunset backstage in almost two decades.

In the dusky light, I shake hands with Johnny Underwood, *The Lost Colony*'s technical director, who runs this year's crew of two dozen actor technicians. His ATs are rehearsing onstage with the rest of the company, so he has time to talk. I have known Johnny, a Roanoke Island native, for more than

*I*n the last year I did the show, 1993, I played Agona. There was this long period in the second act when the choir would sing backstage during Old Tom's parapet speech. As Agona, I would be in the same spot onstage every night. One night, I fixed my attention on the flag that flew from the parapet and started to pick up a pattern. The choir would build to its highest peak when Old Tom said, "Roanoke, O Roanoke, thou hast made a man of me." I started noticing that, at that moment, even if there was dead calm, the flag would whip as if it were being blown by a strong wind. I started looking for it every night, and sure enough, every time at that moment, the flag moved.

— STACEY MAXWELL (1989–93)

thirty years, since he was sixteen. We were both thinner and had more hair back then, and when Johnny carried his surfboard backstage after a day on the beach, the girls sighed as he walked by in his swim trunks. Johnny introduces me to Brandon Cheney, the properties master, a five-year veteran of the show. Together, speaking the shared language of carpenters everywhere, we talk about the show's boat, the only boat I know on the Outer Banks that never goes in the water.

Looking at the masts lying flat on the dock, Johnny tells me how one of them snapped in half during a storm two years ago, how the boat will be twenty-two feet long this year, how the old rusted railroad iron used as a counterweight finally can be retired, and how an AT now is cast specifically to climb the ratlines and wave to the crowd as the boat rolls down the ramp at the end of Act I.

"He also doubles as the dead body at the top of Act II," he says.

As the three of us howl with laughter, the sun emerges from the clouds and floods their faces with amber light. I turn around to look at my sunset, expecting a dull red disk. Instead, I stare straight into a blast furnace.

"I'm blinded," I say, and we laugh even harder. I try to see their faces, but I cannot see anything because in the center of my field of vision is a white void. I see them only peripherally, and as I try to focus, amorphous shapes float around their faces like the ghosts of those who walked these sands more than four hundred years ago.

A perk of spending a summer at *The Lost Colony*: backstage sunsets (Daniel Prillaman in costume as Sir Walter Raleigh). Photo by Jamil Zraikat

Photo by Duane Cochran

After rehearsal, Johnny and I sit in the living room of his A-frame to catch up on old times and old friends. We talk about the new season, and I tell him about seeing ghosts flying around his head.

"You be trippin', Dwayne-O." He grins and sips his whiskey. "Ain't no such thing as ghosts at *The Lost Colony*." And we both burst out laughing.

Among popular theater superstitions is the belief that theaters are haunted by their long-gone actors. And what is now Fort Raleigh National Historic Site was home to 117 men, women, and children who disappeared 430 years ago with England's first attempt to settle the New World; their spiritual presence is almost palpable. I do not consider myself a superstitious man, yet walking the trails alone, late at night, these woods feel spooky, as if my progress were attended by an audience of souls.

The Lost Colony had been my home since fifth grade. I grew up on the sand, playing Wano, fight swing, anything I could. This story is from my third year as an actor technician. It was an exceedingly hot midsummer night, and the sun was just starting to make its way down as I walked back to the gazebo. "Half hour to places everyone! Half hour!" came over the intercom system. I was the last red soldier to get my prop. I fetched the giant awkward thing from its holding spot in the rafters, and as I did the pole kicked out and smacked me in the knee. "F***!" I said pretty loud, rubbed my knee, and picked back up the banner. As I headed towards the open double doors I heard over my right shoulder a deep but light whisper: "Wicked, wicked . . . wicked." I set the pole down and looked around to see if anyone else was with me. I looked under the bleachers, even outside to see if anyone was around the building or possibly underneath. Nothing. I shrugged, picked up the banner, and preset it to its spot stage left. As I crossed that spot where the deck splits I suddenly felt very, very cold. Even now I can't explain that feeling or what I heard. It still gives me the chills.

—— RANDY ALLEN (2001–13)

Pioneers and Dreamers

With The Lost Colony, Paul Green created a new art form, "symphonic outdoor drama."

COMMISSIONED IN 1937 to celebrate the 350th anniversary of England's earliest attempt to establish a colony in the New World, *The Lost Colony* dramatizes the tragic story of those first colonists, culminating with their mysterious disappearance. Before the Pilgrims and Plymouth Rock, before Jamestown and Pocahontas, there was Sir Walter Raleigh's "Cittie of Ralegh" on Roanoke Island, sponsored by his patron, Queen Elizabeth I. In July 1587, some 115 men, women, and children arrived on this wooded, vine-draped island. A month later, Virginia Dare became the first English child born in the New World. By 1590, the wilderness had swallowed them forever, the only clue to their fate being a single cryptic word, *Croatoan*, carved into a tree.

Historical pageants and passion plays were not unknown in America, such as the Pageant and Masque of St. Louis in 1914 and the Florida Historical Pageant in 1922, and regional leaders in North Carolina had been advocating for just such a pageant/drama to mark the upcoming 350th anniversary of the birth of Virginia Dare. Among them were W. O. Saunders, editor of the *Elizabeth City Independent*; D. B. Fearing, a businessman and member of the general assembly; and Mabel Evans, superintendent of the Dare County Schools. In about 1931, inspired by the Passion Play in Oberammergau, Germany, Saunders traveled to Chapel Hill to seek out Paul Green, a Pulitzer Prize–winning playwright and North Carolina native son. Green agreed to attend a meeting at the courthouse in Manteo, at which U.S. senator Josiah Bailey made an impassioned speech urging action. Soon thereafter, the Roanoke Island Historical Association (RIHA) was chartered; to this day, its primary purpose is to produce *The Lost Colony*. Green signed a contract in January 1937 for the script of a show to be staged by July 4 of that coming summer. For his labor, Green was paid the princely sum of fifteen hundred dollars.

Paul Green was a farm boy from outside the town of Lillington in Harnett County. His family was industrious and prosperous, growing cotton and tobacco, as well as corn to feed the hogs they raised for sale. Like farm boys everywhere, he went hunting and fishing, but unlike many he yearned to see more of the world than the backside of the mule pulling the plow in front of him. After graduating from a local academy in 1914, Green taught during the school year, and in the summer he pitched semi-professional baseball to raise enough money to attend college. In the autumn of 1916, over his father's objections, he enrolled in the University of North Carolina in Chapel Hill. Paul's father, a religious man, wanted his son enrolled in a Baptist college; he had read there were atheists in Chapel Hill.

When America entered the Great War in 1917, Paul Green answered the call of duty. He enlisted in the 105th Engineers and after almost a year of drilling and training landed in France. His unit saw heavy combat. He was sent to Officer Candidate School in October 1918, a month before the armistice. A freshly minted second lieutenant, Green was discharged from the army in June 1919. By September, he was back in class in Chapel Hill.

Something astonishing was happening there. In the fall of 1918, Frederick H. "Proff" Koch had blown into town from North Dakota with a sheaf full of plays and a head full of ideas on how to create more. They were what he termed "folk plays," written by his students in Grand Forks, and now that he was teaching in Chapel Hill he wanted more of these plays based on local legends and lore. The university had no theater department, only a drama club that produced amateur theatrics on an improvised stage in Gerrard Hall. A string of footlights was run in front of a temporary apron attached to an elevated platform. The actors entered and exited the backstage area by climbing through an open window.

Proff Koch changed everything. From his own designs, he built a proper proscenium stage in the auditorium of Chapel

Frederick H. "Proff" Koch (left), a professor at the University of North Carolina in Chapel Hill, helped the young Paul Green sharpen his skill as a playwright. They shared a deep appreciation for plays derived from local legends and lore. Photo courtesy of *The Lost Colony*

Director Samuel Selden (left) and Paul Green work on the script for *The Lost Colony*'s 1939 season. Selden directed the play from its original season in 1937 through 1952. Photo: David Stick Collection, Outer Banks History Center

Hill High School. He founded the Carolina Playmakers and in March 1919 presented the first-ever Carolina Folk-Plays, written and acted by his students. One budding actor and writer making her debut was a young woman named Elizabeth Lay, whom Paul Green would marry in 1922. Another actor and writer was a tall, gangly young man named Thomas Wolfe, who would go on to write the novel *Look Homeward, Angel*. When Wolfe died in 1938, Green would be a pallbearer at his funeral.

Paul and Elizabeth Green lived in Chapel Hill, where he continued to write plays that continued to be well received. He still pitched baseball, too. But in 1926, he hit pay dirt when the Provincetown Players produced *In Abraham's Bosom* in New York. It ran for two hundred shows and won Green the Pulitzer Prize for Drama in 1927. In 1931, the Group Theater staged his *House of Connelly* as its inaugural production, to much acclaim. He wrote films and novels and short stories and in 1936 collaborated with legendary composer Kurt Weill for the antiwar play *Johnny Johnson*, winning the Medal of Honor from the New York Drama Study Club. His star shone brightly from coast to coast when he was tapped to write *The Lost Colony*.

In *The Lost Colony*, Green went beyond the original vision for a commemorative pageant to create a new art form, "symphonic outdoor drama," which married all the elements of theater to dramatize a historical event on the very site where it took place. The actual setting was every bit as essential as the script.

The task of designing and building the performance space fell to Albert Quentin "Skipper" Bell, a cigar-chomping English expatriate from the green moors and dales of Yorkshire. A product of trade schools and an assistant to Elizabeth City architect Frank Stick, Bell set about carving Waterside Theatre

Albert Quentin "Skipper" Bell designed Waterside Theatre and supervised its construction by the labor force provided by the Civilian Conservation Corps. Photo: David Stick Collection, Outer Banks History Center

out of a natural ravine at Fort Raleigh National Historic Site on Roanoke Island. Slinging the shovels and axes were a hundred young men from the Civilian Conservation Corps, a work relief program for unmarried men who had trouble finding jobs during the Great Depression.

Skipper Bell certainly knew the balloon framing techniques commonly used in today's residential construction, but he also knew well the older construction techniques that Americans typically visualize as English or Tudor. He knew the post-and-beam construction invariably used in those structures. He knew how to interlace twigs and branches through staked rods before applying concretions to create wattle and daub. He knew how to take reeds from local salt marshes and weave them together to thatch a roof. He knew how to notch logs for cabins, and his log structures became permanent settings onstage with log palisade walls enclosing them. He could build anything, and as mechanic he could fix anything brought to him. Bell also had a green thumb. His nursery on Roanoke Island would provide the first plantings for the Elizabethan Gardens as well as for the theater.

When the show opened on July 4, 1937, more than two thousand people saw *The Lost Colony*, nearly four times the population of Manteo at the time. Among them was *New York Times* drama critic Brooks Atkinson, who wrote a glowing review. To crown the achievement, President Franklin D. Roosevelt attended the show on August 18 of that year during the Virginia Dare Celebration. Today, a plaque marks the spot where he watched from the comfort of his open automobile.

Paul Green's masterpiece is a story of struggle and redemption, defiance and triumph. With a cast and crew of about a hundred, the show is performed in two acts, each of which has six scenes that move between Elizabethan England and the New World. The action begins in 1584 with the arrival on Roanoke Island of English explorers Philip Amadas and Arthur Barlowe and ends with the disappearance of the colonists who landed there in 1587.

The principal roles include historical figures such as Sir Walter Raleigh, the sponsor of the Roanoke voyages; Queen Elizabeth I, England's reigning monarch and Raleigh's patron; Simon Fernando, who piloted the 1587 voyage to Roanoke Island; John White, governor of the new colony; his daughter, Eleanor Dare; and her husband, Ananias Dare, an assistant to the governor. Other principal roles based on historical names include John Borden, a colonist imagined by the playwright as Eleanor Dare's first love and the eventual leader of the colony; Manteo, a chief of the Croatan tribe; and Wanchese, a ruler of the Roanoke tribe. The character Old Tom lends comic relief, especially as he is pursued by Agona. The Historian serves as narrator.

The Lost Colony was intended to run for just one season. Its founders could hardly have anticipated that it would still be performed more than eighty years later.

That first season, *The Lost Colony* drew its talent from Roanoke Island. Today, young hopefuls by the hundreds come from far and wide to audition each year. Director Ira David Wood III and his artistic team compete for talent at auditions sponsored by the Southeastern Theatre Conference and the Institute of Outdoor Theatre and continue the tradition of hosting auditions

I came to *The Lost Colony* through fairly legitimate means: both of my parents, Foster and Marion, were in the show (Mom from '38; Dad after the war). My two oldest brothers, Sean and Gordon, spent infant summers in the barracks at the airport where "the Fitzes" were billeted. My next oldest brother, Terence, was born in October after the last season Mom played the Dame. I grew up hearing semi-mythological tales about *The Lost Colony*, Roanoke Island, the beach and the Beach Club. When my turn finally came in 1974, I jumped at the chance! I was hired by George Trautwein to be in the choir, during the peak of the Layton Years. [It was] a job I loved, respected and joyed-in for the next six summers. . . . In 1975, my mother returned to the Waterside Theatre to play the Queen. In 1976 (bi-centennial year), Dad joined us as Governor White. One of my cherished memories is an image of my dear folks, dressed in their full Elizabethan drag, standing, hands-over-hearts, with the glory of the sunset behind them, as the National Anthem played before the show.

— HASKELL FITZ-SIMMONS (1974–80)

This first appeared on *My Family*, a now-defunct website for *Lost Colony* alumni. It was submitted by Gail Hutchison, a close friend of the late Haskell Fitz-Simmons.

Photo of Carey Blackburn and
Joey Cassella by Jamil Zraikat

in Manteo. Making the effort to drive to local auditions, driving those extra miles, is a good indication of a young artist's determination to be in the show. If you want to be in this show, go to locals.

This season, as in previous years, most of the cast and crew are college kids as green as the pine trees and the plots of tobacco they pass on the drive to the island. Choir members and dancers sometimes come from dinner theaters or theme parks or even cruise ships. Actor technicians usually come straight from class.

But no matter where they come from or what they did before the show, they consider themselves elite, and that "doing the *Colony*" proves they are the best, even if they play small parts with just one line. They play the Burning Girl or the Dead Body or that guy who gets the arrow in the back during the Big Battle, and they play them to the hilt because they are dedicated to the show and incredibly ambitious. If they are lucky enough to land an understudy role, they quickly learn their lines and blocking. When I was in the show, I understudied the Historian and Ananias but never went on. One year, I understudied the Sentinel and went on half a dozen nights. All three roles padded my thin résumé.

These people who make the show happen are the most off-the-wall mix you could ever imagine: unknown actors delivering inspired performances that leave them drained and lifeless; stage-struck wannabes and backstage braggarts dying for their big break; opera singers who have to practice walking and singing so they do not trip over their costumes; show-tune junkies who swap sheet music like romance novels; ballet dancers en pointe; modern and jazz dancers who carry their tap shoes with them wherever they go; technicians who wear nothing but black, even at parties; techs who enter cues on a control board with one hand because they are reading a book from the other. They are all here: the mesomorphs and the runts, the athletic and the willowy, the cerebral and the lowbrow; brooding Method actors with looks so devastating you hope they never speak and ruin the moment; butterfly boys of exact and exquisite poise; young women so excruciatingly beautiful it hurts to look at them.

BACKSTAGE AT *THE LOST COLONY*

Muscle and Hustle

THIS MORNING, HOWEVER, the 2017 cast and crew of *The Lost Colony* look like a legion of the homeless. Standing backstage, eyeballing this year's crop of ATs, I see that these colonists, the "keepers of a dream," to quote Paul Green, hardly look like the heirs to a tradition of excellence; they are the heirs of lousy May weather. Shredded low clouds scroll over the theater. A tepid breeze blows in from the sound, rippling the standing puddles of water and keeping everybody and everything damp. At least the rain stopped.

Even on a day with no wind or rain, with an experienced crew, the setup looks and sounds like the berserker hour.

The actor technicians, all two dozen of them, are milling around backstage in front of the carpentry shop, waiting for morning roll call. As I sit by the door of the men's dressing room, I look down and see scuffed work boots and dirty sneakers, faded jeans and stained sweatpants. Most are dressed in layers since it is still chilly, their hats pulled low and their hoodies cinched tight, so I have to wait for them to look up before I see their eyes. The beards on the young men are coming in, giving them an unkempt look like they are about to ask me for loose change. They exchange soft good mornings in voices no louder than the wind.

This morning, they will not go to work armed with shovels or hammers or wrenches. The shutters and sheets of plywood protecting the windows and doors are down and in storage; the blanket of sand covering the concrete slab of the mainstage lies sifted and spread; the massive Queen's Chamber unit is up in record time. Johnny Underwood told me last night that this morning the ATs will for the first time erect the scenery covering the stage.

The actor technicians are the backbone of the company. Besides performing in the show, they set up, move, and maintain the scenery and care for the props. Photo by Delena Gray Ostrander

Most theaters have a fly loft, allowing scenic elements such as flats to be flown in and out of sightlines on battens. Waterside Theatre does not. At the *Colony*, every stitch of canvas and every stick of scenery must be moved by hand. This action occurs through the wings at mainstage level and via the parapet stairs on the second level. Flats mask the entire stage at the start of the show, and some of them, the greenery flats, are simply huge, requiring a four-person crew to handle them safely. There is no automation backstage; a large, weight-bearing unit such as the Plymouth Ramp must roll on casters, pushed by pure AT muscle through sand that would choke the grooved channels necessary for tracking. When the Queen's Chamber unit swivels, ATs push like Lilliputians opening a giant book. The scenery is expertly designed

BACKSTAGE AT *THE LOST COLONY*

and solidly built, meant to last for years of exposure, and it is heavy—the kind of heavy that can hurt. Most of the flats covering the stage are older than the ATs who will carry them this summer. Wooden ships and iron men. And women, too, you better believe. It blew my mind watching a female AT in a bum roll and a bonnet lead the charge down the parapet steps into the teeth of a nor'easter while carrying a monster flat.

"Today at work call is gonna be weird," I hear a guy say. For new ATs, the setup this morning will be a completely new experience, and they will have to follow the leaders among the returning ATs as best they can. There is no better way.

"We should make a how-to video!" a girl chimes back brightly.

"An orientation video!" declares another guy, like he's hit on a brilliant idea. "Like, 'Have you ever worked fast food?'"

Still another AT says, "Yeah, we'll hire models to play us. Can't you see it?" She pantomimes lifting a flat.

They break into laughter at the thought as Johnny Underwood emerges from the shop where he met with his crew chiefs. He greets his crew casually and calls the roll by first names as they shift their weight from leg to leg and bounce on their heels in anticipation. They rev like engines as Johnny hands out assignments: those who were stage left last year are going stage left this year; those who were stage right go stage right. He gathers all the new ATs and one by one sends them right or left. It looks completely arbitrary, but I know Johnny, and I know he has thought it out. He knows exactly what he is doing.

They begin sliding the scenery out of the scene docks, lugging it onstage and into place, lashing and pinning it down. Together, they groan, the people from exertion and the scenery from old age. But muscles will be built and rust will be knocked off and very soon these people will know this scenery by touch in the dark, six nights a week.

"Preset wreckage," Johnny says.

"Watch the rope," says an AT coiling a line attached to a flat.

> *It blew my mind watching a female AT in a bum roll and a bonnet lead the charge down the parapet steps into the teeth of a nor'easter while carrying a monster flat.*

Together they groan, the people from exertion and the scenery from old age.

"Hands on the handles. One, two, three, lift!" calls a female AT, and a monster flat goes onstage from the wings, four people carrying it.

In front of me, two guys wrangle a parapet greenery flat. They rest it on edge right side up on the deck, and then in one swift motion sling it over their heads until they hold it high, their arms upright, like the Village People spelling the Y in "YMCA." Together, they turn and walk up the parapet steps carrying the plywood and canvas beast.

These beasts have names, too, and not just names designating their assigned spots onstage, like the Organ Covers and the Cabin Covers, but names indicating their shapes, like the A-Frames and the Triangles. Alaska and Canada, named either for their evocative shapes or their immense sizes, perhaps both, flank the Chapel Roof, whose peak is masked by the Cloud, which hangs on steel cables attached to winches backstage. Even on a day with no wind or rain, with an experienced, veteran crew, the setup looks and sounds like the berserker hour. Being backstage is dangerous. Being onstage would be suicidal, so I take a seat in the house and watch the controlled chaos unfold from the safety of a close chair.

An AT calls loudly, "I need two people to go get Skinny!"

I cannot remember which flat that is; maybe it is some code word for a pair of contortionists, like a call for a couple of thin ATs to squeeze tightly in some crevasse of the theater to connect a bolt or lash a line. It would not be the first time.

A couple of guys soon appear, each carrying one end of a thin wall about sixteen feet tall but only about a foot wide, the definition of skinny.

"Watch the Plexiglas part," says an AT as another piece of the Plymouth Wall goes up.

"Grab that chimney," says one AT to another, who immediately picks up one of the two chimneys sitting in the sand, waiting to be installed.

"No, the other one." Followed by, "Didn't you do this last year?"

Their words now come in snatches over the banging and thumping, and they are running, too, going in and out of my field of vision in flashes: I notice a female AT is wearing pink shoes; a male AT has a bright red beard; one has his blue baseball cap on backwards. They shed layers, carelessly wadding up their sweats and jackets and throwing them into the pit or out into the house, carefully avoiding the new green grass in the apron.

"One, two, three, step. And step. And step. And step," says a female voice from behind a cabin cover.

The flat floats up three broad stairs from the sand to the wooden deck in front of Eleanor's Cabin, levitated by the three ATs walking it sideways. The

Daily work calls are a fact of life as an AT in *The Lost Colony*. Photo by Jamil Zraikat

vocalized "step" indicates when to move as one, ascending the individual treads one at a time. The six legs sticking out from underneath the massive flat make it look like a cartoon bug as big as a dinosaur. They do it right; they do it in unison, stepping together as one, giving the impression that the giant green insect is ready to shuffle off to Buffalo or step-ball-change, or at least launch into a tap break.

"Penguin is next," someone calls.

"Penguin goes after Organ Cover," comes the response from the offstage scene dock.

I search my memory for a green penguin with handles on the back and lash lines like dreadlocks. If it relates to the Organ Cover, then it certainly relates to the Step Organ Cover, but I cannot visualize the shape. As I wrestle with my memory, I watch the ATs wrestle with theirs. After some head scratching and fumbling, the little Penguin is found, then single-handedly carried onstage and placed. The ATs all move on except one young woman, who briefly stands in front of it, musing out loud like a mother worried about a weak child: "It's so awkward." She takes a deep breath and says again softly to only herself, "So awkward," then turns to go. Only a returning AT would say something like that.

"I did *not* understand," says a calm, declarative voice from behind Father Martin's Cabin. Obviously, he is new to the game.

The production crew and ATs begin the process of assembling the ship, wrangling it onto the backstage tracks from which it will "sail" during the show. Photo by Duane Cochran

"This is how it works," says Johnny as he walks the AT through the process of locking down Father Martin's Cabin Cover. "You clip it on, then you slide it tight. Clip. Slide. Tight. Got it?"

A crunching, cranking sound issues from somewhere on the other side of the stage as someone yells, "Tie it off there!" I see scenery move and hear, "One, two, three, lift. And step. And step." Then, "Handles down." Now, "Stage left, pull!" I hear a loud series of rattles, followed by a bump, then a loud bang. Every head turns, trying to guess what just hit the deck.

"Don't everybody jump all at once," says Johnny rhetorically, wondering who will be the first to go find out about the big bang. A young woman stands and trots off stage left, saying as she goes, "I want to be helpful."

A disembodied voice high in the greenery on the parapet instructs the ground crew; he's pinning the last flat in place. The people on the ground twist and torque the unruly beast until it is where he needs it to be, and he makes the last pin. Except for the wigwams, which are in the rain shelters being repaired, the stage is set for the top of the show.

"You can come down now," somebody calls to the parapet.

After a pause, I hear the disembodied voice from on high say, "You guys can come up."

Hear Us, O Hear!

I MUST HUSTLE from the theater to *The Lost Colony* Building if I want to be on time for choir rehearsal. The weather is still cool and cloudy, but that will not matter because choir rehearsals are almost always held in the large central room of *The Lost Colony* Building—the LCB—where a dozen folding chairs arc in a semicircle around a brown upright piano. While the dancers sweat under the roof of the gazebo and the ATs toil under the open sky, the singers in the show enjoy the luxury of climate control for their practices. This is not because they are pampered but because the heat and humidity would ruin the upright piano. Still, the necessity of preserving a fine musical instrument from certain destruction in no way mitigates the envy of other company members. When a choir member laments, "I have rehearsal," the comment elicits no sympathy from anyone except other choir members. At *The Lost Colony*, there is no pity for anyone who works in air conditioning, no matter how hard they labor. Just ask a costumer.

As they wait inside for the last of their number to arrive from a costume fitting, a young woman asks, "Does anyone want to hear about my dream last night?" Someone says yes, and she tells how she dreamed that a cast member went into the costume shop, swearing he could fit into Queen Elizabeth's dress, demanding to be fitted in it. When the costumers refused, a fistfight broke out. While the singers laugh, I recall one of Walter Raleigh's lines from the show: "An apt dream, old man."

A door opens behind me and the last singer comes in, dropping his book bag on the floor by the last empty chair. I'm sitting out of the way, but as I look at them I see the men are all growing beards and the women all have their hair tied casually out of their faces. These individuals might have been up for hours,

At The Lost Colony, there is no pity for anyone who works in air conditioning, no matter how hard they labor.

To sing this music proficiently takes vocal heavyweights, masters of tonality and breath control.

but still they look like they just rolled out of bed or came from the gym, and they probably will continue to look this way all through the grueling rehearsal process. Like the ATs I saw this morning, they wear the same uniform and carry the same gear as any colonist: water bottles and notebooks in backpacks, hoodies and flannels at the ready, sensible shoes with no open toes.

Jordan Prescott, the assistant music director, strides out of one of the adjoining offices and goes to the piano, giving his good mornings as he goes. As the choir stands, he hits a single ivory key, and the singers hum to life like an electric motor. The humming rises and falls, dissonant and chaotic, the sounds tumbling and falling over each other in waves.

"Lip trill," he says, and together they sound a chord.

"Step . . . half-step," and the singers respond. They are moving now, swinging their arms and walking in circles to get their blood pumping.

"Slide up . . . and down. Now, hum down on the fifth." He is at the piano, warming them up with arpeggios, the melodious voices rising and falling again, then building higher and higher until he cuts them off.

"Good. High Ds. Come sit." He talks to them about the demands of the music they sing, emphasizing the importance of warming up and stressing the need for true vocal rest, finishing, "We carry our instrument with us, so do things that have a positive influence. We record on Tuesday."

One of the singers raises her hand and says, "I have a super-weird question."

"Then I have a super-weird answer," he replies, and they discuss the alto line of a piece while he plays the piano and she sounds it out to her satisfaction.

"Stand," he says, and they launch into the a cappella opening of Act II.

Singing this music proficiently takes vocal heavyweights, masters of tonality and breath control, so you better have a set of pipes and what I heard a song-and-dance man term "lungs of leather." Breathy, reedy, adolescent voices need not apply for this gig, no matter how sweetly their mothers say they sound, no matter what they're told after church. The show already has enough untrained voices singing off-key or off-tempo. If every tin-eared AT and tone-deaf dancer sang every number in the show, *The Lost Colony* would sound like

For *The Lost Colony*'s original songbook, playwright Paul Green drew from traditional English music. Photo by Eden Saunders, Busy B Photography

a frat party. In my opinion, the reason "Field and Town" from the Queen's Garden scene sounds so good is because the dancers are offstage in the dressing rooms, showering off body paint from the Indian Dance. In the scene, the vocally stronger choir overpowers the ATs because Red Soldiers are onstage—Red Soldiers who are always cast from the pool of ATs. Red Soldiers are not allowed even to speak, much less sing.

There is a reason for the division of labor in the show: while talent abounds, experience is scarce. Just because someone says they love to listen to you sing, or love to see you dance, or love to watch you act, does not mean that your natural talent translates into a substitute for extensive professional training. And training does not translate into experience. While the *Colony* is most certainly a learning experience, it is not an institution of higher learning. Performers must do what they do and do it well, for while an amateur practices until he gets it right, a professional practices until he cannot get it wrong.

"Don't sing." That is what late musical director Roz MacEnulty used to tell people to their faces. I know because that is what she told me in front of the whole company my first year. I was mortified. But I was only nineteen; when I came back four years later, I was good enough for her to sub me into the Prologue choir. It took four years of training and experience for me just to make it that far. Baritones/second tenors like me are a dime a dozen, almost as common as altos, so you can imagine how much further I needed to advance to join the choir full time.

Composer and conductor Lamar Stringfield, founder of the Institute for Folk Music in Chapel Hill, contributed underscoring for the original 1937 production. But most of the music from the original songbook is traditional music from England: madrigals, shanties, hymns, and Anglican chants. That these songs are all in the public domain did not escape Paul Green's notice. After writing plays and films in New York and Hollywood, Green knew his copyright laws well.

Music director McCrae Hardy has introduced original new music into the show and incorporated supplemental sound to make the show more appealing to modern audiences. Photo by Jamil Zraikat

"He pulled out all these public domain English folk songs," said the late playwright's son, Paul Green Jr., when I visited him at his home in North Carolina. "I helped Dad with the music. We drove up to D.C. to do research at the Library of Congress. Dad read sheet music, and I did a little, so he ensconced me in a back room and brought me sheet music, saying 'Copy this' and 'Copy that.' I was Dad's Xerox machine."

In 1967 and 1968, George William Trautwein recorded the show for then-director Joe Layton. Over the decades, a progression of gifted musical directors put their own subtle stamps on the traditional music to keep it from falling flat on modern ears. For the past five years, musical director McCrae Hardy has been updating the choral arrangements. "Some of them sound dated and hokey," he tells me. "They haven't held their age well."

McCrae also introduced new music into the show, music he composed himself, and the addition of this digitally composed and arranged prerecorded music is roughly equivalent to having a live orchestra playing in the pit, something that the originators of symphonic drama could only dream about.

"McCrae Hardy is just incredible," says director Ira David Wood. "One of the most beautiful pieces of music that's come into this show in years has been McCrae's prelude to Act II. It has every musical theme from every piece of music in the show."

Wood continues, "We've looked at the show almost cinematically. [Audiences] are so accustomed to movies and TV and that supplemental sound that you get with the music, so we've incorporated a little more of it into the show, and I think it's had a big effect. It's more theatrical, and I think it helps amplify the emotions of the different scenes."

Wood offers as an example the music that underscores the show's dramatic "Big Battle" scene. "We put music underneath the Big Battle that never was there before. I said [to McCrae], 'Keep the tempo up like a heartbeat. Start it a little slow and then build it, so by the time Manteo and Wanchese are fighting, the tempo is a heartbeat that's faster.' It adds to the tension, it adds to the drama of the scene. . . . So many little things come together to make the big thing work."

McCrae Hardy is not shy about using the backing track either. This year's choir will record in Manteo's Mount Olivet United Methodist Church on Tuesday, and their recorded voices will play under their live performances.

"If I use a backing track, I can layer over it, getting five- or six- or even eight-part harmonies instead of the typical four-part," says McCrae Hardy. "That kind of depth lets me build from something to something else."

The layers of sound also help disguise the fact that the choir is smaller than it has ever been. *The Lost Colony* chorus was originally composed of undergrad students from Westminster Choir College of Princeton, New Jersey, and there were more than two dozen of them each summer, supplemented by local talent. They stood in robes with their songbooks in hand and spent their whole show in a loft on the Queen's Stage, never setting a dainty slipper into the sand onstage. Director Joe Layton put an end to that formality in the early 1960s,

Over the decades, a progression of gifted musical directors put their own subtle stamps on the traditional music to keep it from falling flat on modern ears.

Every summer, *The Lost Colony* choir holds a concert for the community. In 2017, the choir sang duets by Stephen Sondheim. Left to Right; Jordan Prescott (Associate Music Director), Gabe Hoyer, Caitlyn Leach, Gabi Stephens, Tucker Ward, Mila Bolash, Delphon Curtis Jr., Louisa Britt, Kaleb Jenkins, Bethany Johnson, Phillip Rast, Megan Glover. Photo courtesy of *The Lost Colony*

stuffing them into costumes and pushing them out of their loft and onto the stage. As late as 1978, twenty-two men and women were in the choir, and even during my first season there were eighteen. Now, there are twelve.

Back in *The Lost Colony* Building, which houses the show's administrative offices as well as rehearsal space, I listen to the choir sing the music of the show and let my eyes wander the framed photos in the open room. On one wall is a picture from the 1940s: A B-17 sweeps toward the camera, gracefully flying at treetop level over the Chapel of the theater. Across the faded water, Wright Brothers National Memorial is just visible. On another wall is an almost life-sized picture of Manteo and Wanchese fighting in the sand on the beach, both frozen in midair like a still frame from a Bruce Lee movie.

On the wall closest to where I sit is a picture of Marjalene Thomas as Eleanor Dare from the late fifties or early sixties, her smile forever radiant, her eyes forever bright. She looks like the "Swirly Girl," an art nouveau logo of *The Lost Colony* drawn from a commemorative coin struck to finance the show's original production in 1937. She still has the dress that head costumer Irene Smart Rains, known as "Miss Rene," made for her as Eleanor. Old-timers joke that Joe Layton had enough good sense not to replace Marjalene when he overhauled the show in the mid-1960s.

"I was one of the three flower girls in the 1938 production," Marjalene tells me when I visit her at her home on Roanoke Island. "When I was being fitted for my costume, Miss Rene stood me on the table and said, 'Stand still,' but I was about eight years old and I couldn't stop fidgeting and squirming. Finally, she put down her needle and thread and said, 'Marjalene, you've got to stand still. Someday, I'm going to be making an Eleanor costume for you.'"

The layers of sound help disguise the fact that the choir is smaller than it has ever been.

Marjalene Thomas first appeared in *The Lost Colony* in 1938 as a child and has played nearly every major female role in the show, including Eleanor Dare and the Queen. Photo: Aycock Brown Collection, Outer Banks History Center

Creating the Visual Feast

Not a stitch of clothing is wasted; the costumes themselves lead second and third lives.

THE UNFINISHED PLYWOOD FLOOR of the Irene Rains Costume Pavilion is polished not by wax but by the foot traffic going in and out of this large two-story building. I wonder how many people have passed through that door on their way to costume fittings because, except for the permanent Indians, each actor wears more than one costume. An Act I Indian dancer strips off the native garb, showers off the body makeup, and appears in the Plymouth scene Busker Dance wearing a gypsy costume. That same dancer then changes again at intermission into a "good colonist" costume for the Christening Dance and finally into depression rags for Assembly and Final March. Gypsy costumes might be made from old pieces worn during the Pavane Dance. Depression rags are recycled "good colonist" clothes. Not a stitch is wasted; the costumes themselves lead second and third lives.

There is a lot of traffic in the costume shop today. An actor hurries past me on his way back to rehearsal as another enters for his fitting. And while it seems an island of serenity compared with what's happening outside these doors, the fact is that these people are so focused on their work that little conversation takes place. A boom box plays Michael Jackson's "Billie Jean" in the background.

In front of me by the windows that look out on the sound stands a thin young woman bent over a work table. She is dressed in black, and underneath her long black hair I see a pink measuring tape draped around the back of her neck. Looped over her right shoulder is a long, thin band of red ribbon holding a pair of small steel scissors that dangle at her left knee. Her thin fingers fly over a pattern, using a scale ruler and a scoring tool I recognize as unique to her craft. She turns to me and smiles and shakes my hand and returns to her work. Amanda Ferg is the cutter draper, the only one on staff.

In an alcove to the left, two young women sit at a table sewing faux fur onto what looks like a cape. They are the wardrobe stitchers, and the show needs six of them to function. I don't know where the other four are right now, certainly fitting actors for costumes, possibly hanging costumes in the dressing rooms, or perhaps washing and drying one of the mountains of laundry this show produces on any given night. But I know this: they stay busy.

Wardrobe supervisor Kelsey Musselman is in her third season, and she still manages the men's AT and choir room herself. Having been an AT, having spent three seasons in those tight communal accommodations, I admire her bravery. On good days, when everyone has showered and it's not too hot, it reeks like a locker room. On bad days, it stinks like a U-boat; all that is missing is the smell of diesel fuel. Sitting at a desk in the office with assistant shop manager Jeri Meador, she describes her sensory conflict when she carries the basket of dirty T-shirts to the laundry every other night.

"The basket is really heavy because everything is soaking wet with sweat." She rolls her eyes. "And so my arms tell me to hold the basket as high as I can so it doesn't hurt so much, but then my nose gets attacked and my brain tells me to lower the basket, but then it gets heavy again so it goes back up and then down. Up and down, up and down, all the way to the washing machine, my nose and my arms fighting my brain." They both laugh.

Then Jeri says, "And we're not even gonna talk about the Indian bras!" And they laugh even louder.

Backstage, associate designer Brian Mear is painting, or rather repainting, the largest wigwam. He applies brush after brush of diluted scenic paint, distressing the scenery, aging the surface of the earth-tone base coat, then highlighting it with lighter and darker earth tones to give depth. A paint-spattered tarp covers the area under his brush, but the wigwam is bigger, and he must move the tarp every few minutes to keep the paint off the deck.

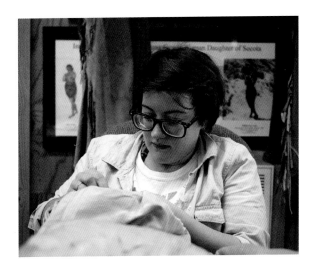

Kelsey Marie, wardrobe stitcher, mends a costume. *The Lost Colony*'s costumers work day and night to care for the costumes and dress the actors. Photo by Jamil Zraikat

The Lost Colony's costumes and sets are designed by William Ivey Long, a six-time Tony Award winner. Photo by Ira David Wood III

"I showed them what to do and asked if they could do it, and they said they could do it," he says, sounding like a parent whose patience is being sorely tested. "I told them, 'Straight lines,' and I come back from lunch and I'm looking at zigzags. It looks like Charlie Brown's shirt." No one is around yet, so I help him carry an A-frame ladder from the back of the women's dressing room. As I walk away, he goes up the ladder to paint the top of the wigwam.

At one of the picnic tables outside the costume shop, two wardrobe stitchers, Chey Wheeler and Caitie Matheny, sit sewing in the shade of the building, working on Ananias's arrow vest and Manteo's cape. Surrealistically, I have never seen these two either apart or without needles in their hands, as if they have sewn themselves together to make conjoined twins. They room together in Morrison Grove, too.

"Manteo's cape has flippy-floppy raccoons. We can't have that now, can we?" says Chey, looping thread through the faux fur.

"We can't have raccoons flapping when he walks, especially when he whips that cape in the Queen's Garden. It could go flying," says Caitie. They both giggle at the thought.

They show me the long, beautifully crafted cape and then the arrow vest. The vest has a spring mechanism built in, allowing a hinged fake arrow to pop up into position when an actor pulls a retaining pin, giving the visual impression that it flew into his back. It's not the only one in the show, but it's on Ananias, and a spotlight will follow him as he fights while wearing the vest, so the vest and mechanism require regular inspection and repair.

The costumers rarely see their work onstage under the lights; they are too busy in the dressing rooms and the quick-change booths to catch more than a few minutes of the show from the wings. Unlike most company members, they also work during the day, constantly repairing and maintaining and replacing the individual pieces listed for their attention at the end of each show. They are the hardest-working people in the show. I cannot imagine what it must have been like before air conditioning.

BACKSTAGE AT *THE LOST COLONY*

"We're rolling, man, we're rolling," says Jonathan Varillas, an AT, as we pass backstage, and the buzz I'm hearing from everyone is good. Even the old-timers—meaning company members who have done the show before—agree it was harder last year. This is a good sign because when the veterans start reminiscing about the show before opening night, it means they have time to think.

Leaving the theater for lunch, I see a familiar figure walking up the asphalt path toward me. That blue blazer, those glasses, those shoes: it can be only production designer William Ivey Long, the lone person I know who has had his own category on TV's *Jeopardy!* *The Lost Colony* is a visual feast because of this man.

With more than seventy Broadway shows to his credit, Long has been recognized with six Tony Awards and seven Drama Desk Awards. He recently completed a four-year elected term as chairman of the American Theatre Wing and in 2005 was inducted into the American Theatre Hall of Fame.

Long's creative talent was nurtured at *The Lost Colony*, where his mother, Mary Long, worked as an assistant costumer with Irene Smart Rains, the show's original costumer designer. Mary Long continued to work in the costume shop even after returning to the stage, playing the character Margery Harvie from 1949 to 1953, then portraying Queen Elizabeth from 1954 until 1963.

His father, William Long Sr., was *The Lost Colony*'s assistant technical director in 1940 and 1941. He returned after World War II as properties master before becoming technical director in 1949, a position he maintained for fourteen years. William Sr. founded the Theatre Department at Winthrop College and directed *The Lost Colony* in 1963. Young William, his brother, Robert, and sister, Laura, were all in the show as kids.

"I would sleep in the fabric bins underneath the cutting tables in the costume shop," Long recalls. He designed his first costume at age six. "It was an Elizabethan ruff for my dog, who stood very still." He credits Irene Rains with encouraging his interest in design and nurturing his talent. A Roanoke Island

I've been a college professor for over twenty-five years now, teaching every theater class my university offers. And it was one short lecture by William Ivey Long that changed my view of theater history. He gave a presentation on the history of *Lost Colony* costumes from its opening until the late 1980s. He showed us how Irene Rains had designed costumes from decade to decade which maintained a core of historical accuracy while also incorporating the silhouette of the fashions of the time! And then he said something that became one of those moments when everything changed. I had been at *Lost Colony* for three years and was on the fence about trying for a career as a professional actor or becoming a college professor. During his presentation, Mr. Long was showing us some costumes from the 1940s, a little tighter in the waists, a little broader in the shoulders. Then he said something to the effect that we were wearing some of those costumes every night. While the colonist outfits in the first act were fairly recent, the depression rags we wore in the second act were actually costumes from decades past! Not only were we performing a play, itself a drama about history, in the place where the history happened, but we were wearing history as well! I realized that *The Lost Colony* is a production, and a place, where the concept of "living history" achieves its truest form. After that season was over, I finished a master of fine arts degree in performance and then decided to continue on to a PhD in theater history. I try to instill in my students a feeling for each era and each production. That's the most lasting gift that *The Lost Colony* gave me: a feeling of being a part of history itself. That was my own fadeless dream.

— GEORGE JACK (1985, 1987–88)

native, Rains studied costuming for several years in New York before becoming an associate professor at the University of North Carolina, where she designed and built costumes for the Carolina Playmakers.

After undergraduate work at William & Mary in Williamsburg, Virginia, Long pursued a master's in art history at the University of North Carolina in Chapel Hill. During his studies, a visiting professor suggested he apply to the Yale School of Drama, where he was accepted. His classmates included Wendy Wasserstein, Christopher Durang, and Paul Rudnick.

Long conquered Broadway, but his memories of growing up at *The Lost Colony* brought him back to Roanoke Island. After seeing director Fred Chappell's show in 1987 during the fiftieth season, he offered to design and was engaged as costume designer the very next year. In 1995, Long's role was expanded to become *The Lost Colony*'s production designer, which extended his creative vision to the sets and scenes.

William Ivey Long with his first mentor, Irene Smart Rains (right), pictured with Pat Kelly Gilbreath as Eleanor Dare in the 1960s. Photo: Aycock Brown Collection, Outer Banks History Center

"I have always had a strong sense of the importance of history," says Long. "My parents, who were both involved in *The Lost Colony* for many years, helped instill this vision in me. I feel that my approach is to use historical knowledge and facts to best tell the story of the Lost Colony through the visual elements of the costumes, scenery, and props."

For Long, a compelling script is the key to keeping audiences engaged. "I am a firm believer that the script should always take the lead in the storytelling," he says. "If the script is strong, the audiences will continue to come and be engaged. That is sometimes hard to do in our age of gadgetry and innovation, but I feel a classic is a classic for a reason, and should not be tinkered with extensively in an effort to woo a modern audience."

That is not to say audience expectations haven't evolved. "Audience expectations have certainly changed over the years," says Long. "What was considered

William Ivey Long based his design for the gown worn by Queen Elizabeth I
(Emily Asbury) on a portrait painted of the monarch between 1592–1599.
Photo by Delena Gray Ostrander

historically accurate in the mid-twentieth century, for example, is no longer the case now that viewers have such a wide range of hyper-realistic films and television programs that have emerged in the last two decades. Good examples of this are the portrayals of Queen Elizabeth I by such notable actors as Dame Helen Mirren, Cate Blanchett, or Dame Judi Dench. These films help show what the modern interpretation of sixteenth-century England looks like. Gone are the days of putting upholstery trim on the hems of skirts and calling them 'of the period.'"

Long is famous for his rigor in researching the periods for which he designs and is especially proud of his costumes for Sir Walter Raleigh and Queen Elizabeth I. "They are based on portraits, and my aim was to make them as accurate as I could, given the harsh conditions under which they are worn six nights per week," he says.

William Ivey Long adjusts the Queen's gown on Nikki Ferry, aided by Hugh Hanson. Photo courtesy of William Ivey Long

William Ivey Long is famous for his rigor in researching the periods for which he designs.

VENDOR/BASKET MAKER
PLYMOUTH SCENE
(ANTHONY CAGE BASE)

JOYCE ARCHAND·FISHNET.

Photos by William Ivey Long

In 1995, William Ivey Long was named production designer for *The Lost Colony*, expanding the scope of his creative role from costumes to the entire show. Photo by Delena Gray Ostrander

In the backstage dressing rooms, costumes share space with the names and messages from those who wore them. Photo by Duane Cochran

William Ivey Long doesn't just make costumes, he makes people, says director Ira David Wood. "Within the beauty of the picture, the suffering and the hardships have to come through as well. Just the look from the costumes in Act I to the peasant costumes in Act II—it's amazing. It's just a subliminal change that you're not necessarily aware of." Wood is referring to the final scenes of the show, which take place on Roanoke Island in the dead of winter. The actors are clothed in wool and clutch their cloaks and shawls under cool blue lights. "It can be a hot August night when there's not breeze enough to float a cloud, but I've seen people [in the audience] adjust their jackets. They actually get cold, they can feel it," says Wood.

CHOREOGRAPHER PAM ATHA is tall and lithe, and she moves about the sound stage with the assurance and confidence of a trained professional with a lifetime of dancing. The sound stage is the same large, low building on pilings backstage behind the women's dressing room that was once known simply as "the gazebo." I had the pleasure of working with Pam many years ago, and to me she is timeless because she makes it look so easy.

The Lost Colony is lucky to have her back. She was in the show in 1978 and in the short-lived, heavily edited touring version that fall. The *Colony* wanted her back as dance captain the next year, but her intent-to-return letter got lost in the mail, so instead of returning to *The Lost Colony* she went on to the big Native American outdoor drama in Cherokee, North Carolina, *Unto These Hills*. Pam spent twenty-seven seasons there at Mountainside Theatre, eventually becoming that show's choreographer. But she is thrilled to be back at the *Colony*, and she energetically and enthusiastically researches and studies the recorded choreography of past seasons, especially the twenty featuring legendary director/choreographer Joe Layton.

When I danced the Pavane in 1987 as an AT, I was informed by then-choreographer Frank Ray that I was cast because I looked arrogant and I fit the costume, not because I could dance. The blow to my ego did not last long because being a Pavane dancer meant I would not be a Red Soldier again, and for that I was truly grateful. The Pavane is a slow processional dance, common in the sixteenth century, that anyone can do if he or she can remember a few steps as simple and repetitive as square dancing or line dancing. Moving well is an ability I lack. Those who can leap and kick and twirl and spin 360 degrees mesmerize me.

"Keep looking at your partner! It will help you in the sand!"

Choreographer Pam Atha leads dancers through a routine during auditions held in Manteo. Photo courtesy of *The Lost Colony*

Pam is working the Indian Dance in the gazebo with the twelve dancers in the company: six male, six female. After her years at *Unto These Hills*, Pam brings a dignity and respect to the dance acquired from dealing directly with Native American sensibilities. The dancers are all barefoot save one, a male who is wearing a pair of white running shoes. It is sunny outside but still chilly, so the dancers wear hoodies and sweatpants over their spandex.

"Girls! You look clustered. Do you feel clustered?" she asks.

"When we're crossing, we're crossing right on top of them," says a female dancer.

"If I give up on the *V*, then I can separate you."

A muted response comes from the dancers, and as I strain to hear it a loud gurgling sound issues from what I assume to be one of the speaker towers onstage, drowning out their voices. It is a strange sound, one I have never heard from a speaker, but before I can process the sound in my head I notice the new flooring in the gazebo, the material something I don't recognize either. The rehearsal starts again.

BACKSTAGE AT *THE LOST COLONY*

*I*n February of 1989, I drove to auditions with some friends who convinced me that after eight years of tap as a small child, I could be a dancer in *The Lost Colony*. I arrived after a fourteen-hour drive in a snowstorm wearing hot pink leotards and purple tights and leg warmers, and my hair was bigger than my car. I'm thinking, I think I can fake this. Marie Evans, who was leading the dance audition, starts calling out ballet terminology, at which point I am completely lost. After fifteen embarrassing minutes, Marie patted me on the back with a look that seemed to say, I'm really sorry, but there's no chance in hell. A few weeks later, I went to the Southeastern Theatre Conference auditions—my first major auditions—with my heart set on *The Lost Colony*, but I didn't get a callback. Still, I was determined to do the show, so I paced around outside the room where Fred Chappell and Bob Knowles were auditioning the actors on the callback list. I walked up to the door and wrote my name on the list, hoping they would be willing to just talk to me. Eventually, Fred opened the door, and I introduced myself, apologized profusely, started name-dropping, talking about how much history I knew, and finally asked, "Can I be an actor tech?" Fred probably thought I was insane. I was sure I'd blown it. The next morning, getting ready to drive home, I saw Fred Chappell standing in the hotel lobby with a suitcase. "Mr. Chappell, I just want to thank you," I said. "Honey, I just put your contract in the mail," he replied.

—— STACEY MAXWELL (1989–93)

In addition to choreographing the show, Pam Atha (center) played the role of Dame Coleman in the eightieth anniversary season. Photo by Eden Saunders, Busy B Photography

"Back up!" Pam says as the dancers set. "Give yourselves room to travel."

She turns on the playback, and they begin. I recognize much of what is done, if for no other reason than that I saw her choreography last year. But then it happens: fish hands. The dancers shimmy and shake their hands like swimming fish; it has always been my favorite part of the ensemble routine. The action builds into work I don't recognize.

"You don't have to jeté so far!"

The featured dancer in the show is the medicine man Uppowoc, which in the Algonquian tongue means "tobacco." As that dancer, Christopher M. Flores, enters, all focus falls on him. He is a magnificent dancer, and with great leaps he bounds across the floor. Once again, I sit mesmerized, imagining Nijinsky's *Afternoon of a Faun*, but when I ask Pam about that during a break she tells me her work is based on a Green Corn Dance performed by Native Americans. Since the dance is not a sacred rite, she feels free to utilize it during the show, but she tells me sacred dances are taboo.

The Christening Dance with its paddle turns is next. The dancers are sweating now, peeling off outer layers and wiping their faces with them. The male dancer wearing white running shoes kicks them off with a flourish at Uppowoc, who is sitting cross-legged in a corner, and the shoes lightly bounce off him, landing on the floor. It is either a harmless tease or a gentle taunt, and although I don't know them I suspect they are like two schoolboys on the playground who punch each other in the arm to see who will say "Ouch!" first.

Pam counts off, "Five and six and seven and eight . . ."

I look around to see if I can find a better place to watch, but just as the dance starts there is a jarring thud. A dancer has fallen. The action stops, and I look to see who fell; it is the dancer who kicked off his white running shoes

at Uppowoc. He is up before the ten count, walking it off like an athlete while the other dancers crowd around him, gently stroking him and holding his hand. When he kicked off his shoes, he hadn't stripped off his socks, which is probably what made him slip and fall. He will certainly sport a big bruise in the morning. Pam studies him like a mother who has warned a little boy over and over not to stick his finger in a light socket, only to watch him do exactly that.

"Are you okay?" she asks him.

"I'm soooo good," he says.

"Good," she responds curtly, and they launch back into Christening. It is a joy to watch.

The lead dancer performs the role of the medicine man Uppowoc. In 2017, Uppowoc was played by Christopher M. Flores. Photo by Delena Gray Ostrander

I was in New York taking a class. John Lehman, the choreographer, and his wife spent the winter there; he was working on his skills as a choreographer. And he started thinking maybe he could get a couple of professional dancers to come down from New York. When class was over, he came up and introduced himself and asked if I had any interest in being in a show in North Carolina, and I said, "Tell me more," and we spoke for an hour. He described the show a little bit but spent a lot of time describing the people and the area, and he didn't exaggerate one bit. Everything he told us about the production, the charisma about it, and the people—it was all true. He said, "This place has been isolated. They're not used to having strangers in their midst." Because even people from inland North Carolina would have been strangers, but we were damn Yankees. John Lehman encouraged us to be modest and very respectful and to regard ourselves as guests in their community. In those days, there was just the beach road with nothing on it. There were only five hundred people in the town. So when John said the show often played to two thousand people, I didn't believe him. But sure enough, he didn't exaggerate one bit.

— EDDIE GREENE (1953–54)

"Kick! And *kick* the other leg!" she calls to the dancers. *"Don't trot!"*

A male dancer, reveling in the moment, yells to no one in particular, "We're *elegant!*"

"Keep looking at your partner! It will help you in the sand!"

When it is over, everyone is breathing heavily, but they are not panting; that will come later. All the hoodies and sweatpants lie in piles on the floor. As they catch their breath, they show the energy and exuberance of youth. One of the male dancers picks up another male dancer and holds him upside down. Only a dancer could be this casual and relaxed about his body around others.

"They take it for granted," Pam says with a smile, shaking her head.

During the lunch break, I go to see retired choreographer Johnny Walker at his home in Manteo. In the wet spring air, the landscaped grounds of his large, rambling house are a riot of life where hundreds of decorative plantings have matured, creating rooms of hydrangea and crepe myrtle beneath the pines and live oaks. Little paths lined with flowers and herbs connect the rooms: here stands a trellised entrance; there sits a low bench. A piece of statuary on a pedestal graces a corner, and tall, glazed ceramic urns hold the newest plantings of the year. Johnny tells me that he needs these tall pots now. His knees are too bad for him to work comfortably on the ground.

Johnny first danced for the show in the summer of 1964 as an eighteen-year-old theater major from East Carolina University in Greenville. He had never taken a dance class in his life.

The featured dancer in the show is the medicine man Uppowoc, which in the Algonquian tongue means "tobacco."

Edward Greene was among the first professional dancers to be recruited from New York City by then-choreographer John Lehman. Photo: Aycock Brown Collection, Outer Banks History Center

"I auditioned in Chapel Hill at the Institute of Outdoor Drama and got the job," he reflects. "And then I learned some-one else was making five dollars more a week than me, so I started hitchhiking out 264 from Greenville to Manteo. It was ten o'clock at night, and I was scared as hell when a preacher and his wife pulled over. They were on their way back from a revival. Bless them, they took me into their house, fed me and gave me a bed, and the next morning drove me across Mattamuskeet to 64, where I hitched a ride to Manteo with somebody going to buy plants at Skipper Bell's nursery. When I auditioned again, Joe Layton heard the whole story and said, 'Give him the five bucks'! And that first summer, I made forty-eight dollars a week."

He and I are sitting at his dining-room table now, and as I look about the room I notice that the inside of his home resembles a reverse image of the yard. Outside, the few sculpted pieces of art punctuate the innumerable plants, but on the inside the accumulated statuary, carvings, textiles, paintings, and ceramics overflow every wall and shelf and corner, while individual plants accent the room. Both scenes are strikingly beautiful, as complementary and as contradictory as a photograph's vivid color print laid side by side with its inversely colored negative.

"Joe based the Indian Dance on a piece by the Ballet Folklorico de Mexico. Both the deer solo and the fish solo were based on that. Walter Stroud danced Uppowoc my first year, and Michael Penta danced it in '65. I was still attend-ing ECU on a fellowship when I was invited to be one of the original students at the North Carolina School of the Arts in the fall of 1965. I danced Uppowoc first in 1966." He laughs and says, "At the cast party after the show in '66, Joe pulled me onto his lap and said, 'You don't know this, but you danced as beau-tifully tonight as I have ever seen anyone dance.' Joe never forced choreography on a body that couldn't handle it. He made the Ralph Lane Dance an adagio solo. It was about control."

"What do you mean, 'adagio'?" I ask.

"Slow. Joe was very conscious of the rhythm of the show, and he wanted the pulse of the show to slow during that dance, before Ralph Lane attacks. And Joe was very conscious about how knowledge gets passed down. You need to

prepare these people, prepare them for that large a space. The space and the sand." Then he bursts out laughing. "They don't know how to plié in the sand."

After he stops laughing, he confides, "It's about preparing for the future, about passing knowledge down."

Driving away, I wonder how many dancers Johnny Walker has prepared for the future. Then I think of the plants around his house. He patiently tends those living things, nursing them in the Roanoke Island soil, watering and pruning them when necessary, until one day they burst into bloom. He has more than I can count.

But I can count the dancers in the show this year, and just like the choir there are fewer than previous years. Old programs in my hotel room tell me there were at least half again as many, but unlike the choir, dancers cannot be recorded for a backing track.

Dancing in the sand requires special conditioning and technique. Photo by Eden Saunders, Busy B Photography

Light and Sound

"It's all about achieving a balance between power and control."

AT AN EVENING REHEARSAL, after two days of searching, I finally find the electricians huddled at the production table. I missed seeing them during daylight because they are working late at night, after the actors and other technicians have left, when they have the empty theater for themselves. Conspicuous signs of their labor are everywhere: rehearsal lights are up and working; show lights hang in the towers and wings; coils of thick black cable litter the top of the hill, their lengths indicated by small colored flags of tape; the concrete to one side of the two-story "light shack" is crowded with assorted lighting instruments in various states of repair and assembly; gel frames lie scattered in small piles. To a casual observer, this whole picture might be mistaken for the scrap metal collection point at a local recycling center. Nothing could be further from the truth. Instruments must be cleaned, shutters must be lubricated, and electrical connections must be tested before some young man or woman in a rigging harness hangs lights safely in their positions. The lights are hauled up manually, hand over hand, on a sturdy synthetic rope with a bowline tied on the end. Once installed, they may have gels for color or gobos for pattern.

Lighting designer Josh Allen tells me about the show in 1991, his first year as an electrician. The light board was technically known as a Strand Mantrix seventy-two channel two-scene preset analog lighting console.

"It was as long as a coffin," he says, spreading out his arms. "And the guy with the longest arms ran it." Then he launches into technical jargon that sails over my head. While it hasn't been that long since I worked on what roadies term "dimmer beach" and "monitor world," I haven't kept up with technology, so I ask him to dumb it down for me.

"It's all about achieving a balance between power and control," he explains.

"We use the control cables to set levels and . . ." Then I'm in over my head again, so I gently change the subject and ask him what kind of lighting board the show has now.

"Now, we have an ETC Gio @5, so instead of seventy-two analog channels we have . . ." He turns to his crew and asks, "Who's got a calculator?"

Noah Trimner, the assistant designer, and Bri Weintraub, the master electrician, both pull out their phones.

"What's 512 times 128?" asks Josh.

"It's 65,536," says Bri.

"Yeah, we used to have 72 channels, and now we have 65,000."

"It's 65,000 *and* 536," says Bri.

"If we need them," adds Noah after a pause.

"Yeah, if we need them," Josh echoes as they all laugh.

Bri is wearing a black toboggan with a battery-powered LED sewn or hot-glued onto the front of it. She explains that the tiny light enables her to see into both the darkest corners of the theater and the tightest seams of the instruments. I ask if she made it herself.

"No, but I should rebuild it. It would be way better."

It's spitting rain in the theater. A north wind blows off the sound, but it is not cold. The scenery and props for the top of the show are preset; the lights in the towers are up and throwing bright light onto the sand onstage as Jake Newcomb, the sound engineer, does his mic check from the sound booth at the top of the hill.

"Turn your pack down six dBs," he says to the actor wearing mic number eleven. The spotlights are on now, ballyhooing around the stage in sweeps as the operators check their range of motion. One of the spots points to the actor as she walks offstage, then picks up the next as he comes to center.

"Number seventeen," barks the actor. "Aye, Simon! Speak it out, Simon! We're with ye!" The actor's voice is loud and strong. He repeats his lines several times, each time building in volume.

"Nice projection," Jake says to him loudly. Then, under his breath, he says,

A tangle of lighting equipment waits to be sorted out by the electricians. Photo by Ira David Wood III

To a casual observer, this whole picture might be mistaken for the scrap metal collection point at a local recycling center. Nothing could be further from the truth.

"That's why we have compressors." A few of the production staff have heard him, however, and laughter trickles through the house as another actor comes onstage.

"Number ten." He takes a breath and says, "And it would be the food of slaves!" But we can hardly hear him.

"Ooo! It might be off," says Jake. "Continue. I'm working on the levels." He concentrates on his controls while the actor repeats his line over and over until it becomes comical.

"And it would be the food of slaves! Did I happen to mention that it would be the food of slaves? Because it would be the food of slaves! Food of slaves! How many times do I have to tell you it would be the food of slaves?"

"Thank you," Jake says to the actor as the pyrotechnician crosses the stage with his arms hugging several guns.

"Number twenty, Elizabeth Lane," says an actor. "Girl? But we are praying it will be a boy." She has a clear, sweet voice and repeats her line several times, each time sounding the same, until it becomes a song in my head. Then she changes, wailing, "Let us leave this cursed place!" repeating it again and again with the same inflection as Jake fiddles with the dials.

He cocks his head for a moment, listening, then takes a deep breath and sighs, "I love it when the bugs calm down."

The master electrician appears onstage and immediately turns about face, peering up into the wings, squinting into the lighting instruments, confirming they are working, repeating the word *Check* into her wireless headset as she counts down their numbers. Her long blond hair whips around her, marking the spot where she stood a split second earlier, following in the wake of her constant movement as she weaves and bobs like a boxer.

"Clear," she announces, and then the stage is suddenly empty, save for the wigwams and the flats and the totem poles. I see five smaller, man-sized totems around the large central one, and it strikes me as odd; I thought there were six. I look more closely and see where the sixth should be. It has been replaced by a large wooden-handled push broom sticking out of the augured hole in the sand. The totem pole is still backstage, under repair.

Sound design for *The Lost Colony* is a tricky business, given the big stage and amphitheater, the need to blend recorded sound with live singing, and ambient noise surrounding the outdoor venue.

Instead of trying to mask the ambient sound, sound designer Michael Rasbury finds ways to use it to the show's advantage, as he's done with the sound of dogs barking near the theater. According to director Ira David Wood, Rasbury recorded them. "And what we do is we add the dogs barking at certain spots in the show, a couple of places where we're controlling it, so when they do bark for real it's not distracting," says Wood. "It's a very small, little subliminal thing, but it's incredible."

Rasbury also incorporates sounds occurring naturally in the environment to set the mood and enhance the performance. Explains Wood, "Rasbury can take [the sound of] an owl and put it up in a tree because the speakers now can separate the sound. And so when you hear an owl hooting in a tree off in the background, it sounds real. We have the waves slapping at the very beginning, and the sound of seagulls in the distance. People listening to that will think they're hearing the Roanoke Sound. But it's recorded. So you're actually taking control of the environment, and you're making it work theatrically for you."

Sound is used in other subtle ways to enhance the aesthetics and mood of the show. "We've added this low wind in Act II, so you constantly hear in the background the sound of cold wind blowing across the water in the winter-time. And psychologically, you feel cooler," says Wood.

Sound design for *The Lost Colony* is complex, incorporating multiple speakers and audio channels and live and recorded sound—a blend of technology and artistry. Photo by Duane Cochran

The Lost Colony experience improves with each year. It is an accomplishment that bears witness to the people of Manteo, who refused to let it die in spite of hurricanes, fires, and financial difficulties. It bears witness to those with talents who come every year to compete for the opportunity to perform. It honors those millions of people across eighty years who have made their pilgrimage to sit for two hours and watch those colonists come alive and then disappear right before their eyes. It is hard to leave the experience untouched, and its effect can linger and continue for many years. Nineteen sixty-seven was the last time I got to attend a performance. But I have wished every year I could be there again, and in my heart I am. During each season near sunset, I sit on my porch and think about a new performance getting ready to start. I am proud to be one of the "keepers of a dream."

— DR. JEAN B. GEARHART, faithful audience member

Breathing Fresh Life into a Sacred Script

"I TELL THEM THEY'RE CRAZY," says the show's director, Ira David Wood III. He means the whole company. "I tell them they're all crazy because they could be working indoors in an air-conditioned theater doing four musicals instead of sweating in the sand, doing the same show six nights a week."

Wood ought to know. He joined the show in 1968 when he was a student at the North Carolina School of the Arts and played the principal roles of Sir Walter Raleigh and Old Tom. After leaving *The Lost Colony*, he went on to a successful career in film, television, and stage. His original production of *A Christmas Carol*—cited as one of the most successful shows in North Carolina theater history—has been performed every December in Raleigh for forty-three years. But the director calls his time with *The Lost Colony* the best years of his life.

Working with director Joe Layton had a profound influence on Wood. "I've sat at Joe Layton's feet. I probably ended up annoying him, I was asking so many questions about why he was doing what he was doing. I learned [from Joe Layton] everything I know about making pictures on the stage, and moving people into those pictures, and how important the pictures were in terms of evoking responses from the audience."

He continues, "In the old days, when people had love scenes or death scenes, they would play them on stage left because that was the side where the heart was. The villains always came

Director Ira David Wood III performed in *The Lost Colony* from 1968 to 1970, playing the principal roles of Sir Walter Raleigh and Old Tom. As Old Tom, he played opposite Cora Mae Basnight, who held the role of Agona from 1957 to 1982. Aycock Brown photo courtesy of *The Lost Colony*

"These are some of the most beautiful words that I've spoken on the stage."

on stage right. It's the side farthest from the heart. In a cast of almost a hundred people, everybody has to be in the right place to evoke the right emotional response."

Even as a young actor, Ira David Wood knew he wanted to direct *The Lost Colony*. "When I left the show in 1970, I called Paul Green and said, 'I'm going to direct the show one day, and I think that you won't be here. Do you think that it's presumptuous of me to talk to you about some ideas about the show?' And he loved it. One of the things that I mentioned to him was the fact that I wanted to see Eleanor take a gun and shoot an Indian during the battle. He loved that idea. Audiences today see the evolution in Eleanor, from a refined lady of Queen Elizabeth's court to a strong woman who is up to the struggle of settling in a strange new land."

Wood's first instinct as artistic director was to return to the Joe Layton production. "There had been so many directors, so many changes in the show. The first thing I wanted to do was to return it to what I remembered when I was an actor. And we did, and I think the best compliment we got was from the locals who said, 'You gave us back our show!'"

He also confronted the reality that audience tastes had changed since 1970. "People would sit for three and a half hours and watch a Broadway show. They just don't do that anymore. That was the challenge."

For years, Paul Green's script had been sacrosanct, but Wood found the RIHA Board of Directors amenable to judicious pruning. He assured the board members he revered the playwright's script and would prune carefully. "I love these words. These are some of the most

Director Ira David Wood III (center) runs through a comic bit with Robert Hooghkirk as Old Tom (left) and Kole Mitchell McKinley. Photo by Jamil Zraikrat

Joe Layton (right), *The Lost Colony*'s artistic director from 1964 to 1984, is widely credited with revitalizing the outdoor drama, reworking the script in close collaboration with playwright Paul Green. Layton's production was a source of inspiration to Ira David Wood III when he returned in 2013 to direct the show. Layton is shown here with Bob Knowles, who was hired in 1969 as production coordinator and served as general manager from 1980 until his retirement in 1993. Photo courtesy of *The Lost Colony*

beautiful words that I've spoken on the stage," he says. "The best compliment that I had from former company members was, 'We know you cut it, but we don't know where.'"

Preserving *The Lost Colony* for future generations is a goal in keeping with Wood's philosophy of giving back. "It always stuck with me that you have to give something back. I learned so much here. I want to bring the show up to the level of perfection I know it can be."

Ultimately, Wood believes the key to a quality show is having a good return rate from previous years. "We're building a family, not a cast," he says, then adds, "Thank God for the locals."

Opening Night

How many colonists does it take to change a light bulb? All of them: one to change the bulb and the rest to talk about how they did it last year.

ON OPENING NIGHT, my wife, Elizabeth, and I drive from our rented cottage in Manteo to Waterside Theatre and park at *The Lost Colony* Building. The main lot will be jammed with vehicles of all sizes, and a commuter's smug satisfaction creeps over me at the thought of having evaded the traffic; also, when I park here, I will not have to worry about careless children darting in front of me from behind parked cars. Company members used to be required to park here during the show, leaving every space in the big lot for the paying public, and while some cars are parked on the paved loop and the grass infield, they seem fewer than I remember from years ago. The air is cooling now after a hot, sunny day, and the early evening is mostly clear, with a few tall clouds creating a dramatic but unthreatening sky. Sunset will be beautiful.

Elizabeth and I walk together on the narrow concrete path into the woods, turning and passing the earthworks of the restored fort on our right. The crowd from the main parking lot is in front of us now, moving as one from right to left under the live oaks and Spanish moss, walking into the theater.

We have good seats down low, seats that will be easy to reach, and we have plenty of time before the seven-thirty curtain. Under the rain shelter near the concession stand, I see a stall selling souvenir key chains and refrigerator magnets, along with plastic bow and arrow sets and wooden swords.

The setting sun throws gold light on the white clouds as a recorded announcement welcomes us to the theater. We take our seats by the Queen's Stage, where a microphone and stand are preset. Presently, three men enter the stage and in turn make short welcoming speeches to inaugurate the eightieth

One of my favorite moments from my two seasons with the *Colony* was during the 2016 production. The Fallen Sentinel was part of my track that year. I would go to my place just behind Eleanor's Cabin, and by that time the Big Battle had ended so the whole theater was enclosed in a serene sort of calm. Then I would make my way up to the parapet and take my post with my back to the audience, looking out over the sound. I did this every night in all sorts of weather, from blazing hot and muggy to freezing cold and windy. But looking out over Roanoke Sound with the lullaby being sung in the background, no matter what the conditions, was one of the most peaceful moments of the show for me. In many ways, it was also therapeutic. I have yet to find something else that replicates it. The only word that can describe it is magic, in its best and purest form.

— NICHOLAS C. PARKER (2014, 2016)

anniversary season of *The Lost Colony*. Their remarks are both worthy and commendable, and we join the polite applause following each one, but my anticipation is insufferable as I wait for the show to start.

The show opens with a prerecorded audio montage of key lines spoken by the actors. With original music by musical director McCrae Hardy swelling underneath, the narrator of the show—the Historian, costumed as a park ranger—enters slowly from the woods on the Indian Stage. This character will guide us through the show, stitching together time and place.

Greeting the audience directly, speaking additional lines written by director Ira David Wood, the Historian, played by Don Bridge, draws us into his confidence, saying he has come to watch the sunset. He is folksy and humble, far from the ecclesiastical Historian of Joe Layton or the supernatural Historian of Fred Chappell. But once he has the audience in his hands, he changes gears adeptly, saying a short prayer penned by Paul Green, ending with an amen. Reflexively, the audience members reply with an amen of their own, and the bond of trust is established.

It is ridiculous to suggest I have no expectations of the show, since I took part in approximately 350 performances. The Historian is one of the few characters on whom the director can put his conceptual signature. In theater, there is a saying: "It's all about choices." Over the thirty-four years since I first worked the show, I have seen many choices made on this sand, some good, some better. I am not a critic of the show, and director Ira David Wood's choice to make the Historian into a park ranger works. I think it works primarily because the man playing the Historian, Don Bridge, whom I have had the pleasure of knowing for many years, is a chatty, understated kind of man in real life. A versatile actor with a broad range, he is perfect for the concept of this role.

The Historian leads us into the Indian Dance, and the show goes on from there.

Of all the principal characters in Paul Green's script, directors have the most discretion in how they portray the Historian, whose narrative helps the audience understand the history driving the action on stage. In 2016 and 2017, Director Ira David Wood imagined the Historian, played by Don Bridge, as a park ranger. Photo courtesy of *The Lost Colony*

Elizabeth and I talk about what we like and what we do not like, but those are merely our opinions. For example, after the show, when I mention that I did not care for one actor's performance, she vehemently disagrees. I am reminded of a favorite joke among *Colony* people: How many colonists does it take to change a light bulb? All of them: one to change the bulb and the rest to talk about how they did it last year.

The only opinions that really matter are those of the people who pay their hard-earned money to see the show. Tonight, those people are not looking off into space or squirming uncomfortably in their seats; they are watching every scene. This tells me somebody is doing something right, just as when I see actors working so hard onstage, I know they cannot fail with the weight of the show behind them. It will be a good season.

At intermission, I see an older couple sitting a few seats in front of us. He stands first and as he is stretching asks her, "Well? Whadaya think?" She silently nods her head in approbation.

After I go to the concession stand for more soda and popcorn for Act II, two young boys hurry to get back to their seats before the lights go out. "This is better than pirate school!" says one as they race past me with their arms flapping, like they could grab the air and pull themselves along faster than they already are going.

The eightieth anniversary season attracted significantly more theater-goers than *The Lost Colony* had seen in several years. Photo courtesy of *The Lost Colony*

Slaughter

These people are cutting loose, shedding three unbroken weeks of focus and tension in one night's revels.

WHEN THE SHOW OPENED on Friday, the VIPs had wine and hors d'oeuvres served sound-side before the show. Now, it's Saturday night after the show, and the actors are congregating in Morrison Grove, the apartment complex that is home for almost everyone in the show. Tomorrow will be their first day off since the initial company call three weeks ago. After three weeks of nonstop work, the show is up and running, and tonight everyone is getting Slaughtered.

"Slaughter" is the name of the cast's opening party, originally "Slaughter of the Innocents," the "Innocents" being the first-time company members. I have seen some wild ones in my time. But almost immediately after tonight's show, the heavens opened with a vengeance, drenching the brown paper bag luminaries that line the entrance to the Grove and washing away the ex-company members who stay up late to welcome everyone into the fold. Usually, the old-timers hold a candle-lighting ceremony, passing the torch, as it were, to the newest initiates to *The Lost Colony* experience. Tonight, because of the thunderstorm, that ceremony is postponed.

"I've never seen a Slaughter rained out," says Robert Midgette, fight director for the show. Robert's family roots run deep on these islands, since at least 1784, when a written deed in Currituck attests to the ownership of a tract of land by his ancestor Lewis Midgett. "We've had thunderstorms before, but they came later, after the party had started."

Robert and I are sitting in the living room of the National Park Service A-frame house where Johnny Underwood lives. Johnny is Skyping with his girlfriend, Stephanie, in Atlanta, and the rain is tapering off, so Robert and I decide to drive to the Grove. Johnny says he will follow later on his bicycle.

In the parking lot of the Grove, I hear the party as soon as I step out of the car, and I hurry to Robert's side as he walks up the path. Robert is a current company member, and while I know Morrison Grove from my summers living here, I am essentially an outsider to the cast and crew of the eightieth season. I need a wingman or I will be shunned faster than a used car salesman at an Amish barn raising, so I stick close to Robert, sipping soda out of my big red and white souvenir cup, trying not to spook the guys or creep out the girls. Eventually, I calm down and relax after I realize nobody cares about anything right now except getting Slaughtered.

In front of me in the center of the Grove, a big grill cooks burgers and dogs, and properties master Brandon Cheney tends it with a smile. Strands of party lights festoon the trees, and upbeat music pounds from speakers somewhere. A couple of kegs flow over to my left, where a bearded young man pours sudsy beer into a red plastic cup. One folding table has paper plates next to a big bowl of potato salad, alongside chips and dip. Another table has a punch bowl and another some sort of bar with liquor and mixer bottles in various stages of emptiness. The noise is overwhelming; in the center of the Grove, the music assaults me in waves as it bounces off A, B, and C Buildings.

These people are cutting loose, shedding three unbroken weeks of focus and tension in one night's revels. Exhaustion and alcohol will eventually put them to sleep, and sleep late they will, but nobody in this crowd is thinking about that right now.

I always tell the kids in the show, "Look, in twenty or thirty years, you're going to be sitting in a restaurant somewhere—it could be in California, New York, or Timbuktu—talking with friends and saying, 'That reminds me of my days in *The Lost Colony*.' And someone sitting five tables over will say, 'Were you in *The Lost Colony*? I did the show, too!'" Once you've done the *Colony*, you're a part of a very big family.

— HUNT THOMAS
(1969–73, 1976, 1992–96, 2009)

Scenes from *The Lost Colony*

In the Prologue, members of the choir emerge from the trees dressed in the ragged colonist costumes also worn in the final scenes. Photo by Delena Gray Ostrander

The Lost Colony's portrayal of the Algonquian tribe is informed by drawings Governor John White made during the 1587 voyage to Roanoke Island. Photo by Delena Gray Ostrander

In the colorful Queen's Garden scene, Queen Elizabeth I (Emily Asbury) samples tobacco as her court and Algonquian Indians Manteo and Wanchese look on. Manteo (Joey Cassella, left) and Wanchese (Philip Culton) did indeed sail to England with Arthur Barlowe and Thomas Harriot in 1584, where they were hosted by Sir Walter Raleigh. They returned to present-day Roanoke Island in 1585. Photo by Delena Gray Ostrander

The Queen's court leans in. Left to right: Landon Ferrell, Riya Braunstein, Jane Kiley Simmons, Jessica Burrell, Wyatt Daniel Neff. Photo by Eden Saunders, Busy B Photography

Director Ira David Wood III introduced a passionate kiss between John Borden (Ethan Lyvers) and Eleanor Dare (Henson Milam) to heighten the expression of their emotional bond. Photo by Delena Gray Ostrander

The first fight occurs in a brief scene in the first act, when Ralph Lane and his men attack the peaceful Indians. Here, the medicine man Uppowoc (Christopher M. Flores) mourns the death of King Wingina. Photo by Delena Gray Ostrander

Simon Fernando (Jamil Zraikat), the Portuguese pilot who sailed on three voyages to Roanoke Island, is characterized as a villain who abandons the colonists on Roanoke Island, a portrayal based on the writings of Governor John White, father of Eleanor Dare. Photo by Eden Saunders, Busy B Photography

When casting the principal roles, Director Ira David Wood looks for actors with the skill, physicality, and charisma to occupy Waterside Theatre's large stage. A commanding presence is a prerequisite for the role of Queen Elizabeth I (Emily Asbury, shown here with Daniel Prillaman as Sir Walter Raleigh, right, and Terry Edwards as Governor White). Photo by Delena Gray Ostrander

The colonists celebrate the christening of Virginia Dare, the first English child born in the New World, the historical event that inspired the show. Photo by Eden Saunders, Busy B Photography

In the second act, the comical character Old Tom (Robert Hooghkirk) undergoes a transformation from bumbling drunkard to a self-described "man of parts in the wilderness" who informs Eleanor Dare (Henson Milam) of his plans to wed the Indian maid Agona (Patsy Hart). Photo by Eden Saunders, Busy B Photography

The Lost Colony's final scenes can be poignant moments for both the actors and the audience.
Photo by Delena Gray Ostrander

TWO

Sustaining the Fadeless Dream

During our first evening together, I spoke of those who sleep beneath these sands . . . and of the responsibility we owe to them, their memories, and their Dream. My then-expressed prayer was that, amid the youthful joy and partying spirit that is also part of this experience, you would also give those souls some bit of continued immortality by dedicating a few precious moments of your backstage time to consecrating thoughts and heartfelt reflection. During my occasional sunset strolls behind the scenes, I see you drifting off to quiet places . . . one at a time . . . here and there . . . by yourselves . . . or with each other . . . *and I know.* What is more important and lasting is the fact that *they* know . . . and because of *you*, they live again . . . as does their sacred Dream.

— DIRECTOR IRA DAVID WOOD III,
in a letter to the cast and crew of
The Lost Colony at the start of the
eightieth anniversary season

Photo by Delena Gray Ostrander

Settling in for the Summer

Opening night fixes life for the next three months.

OPENING NIGHT HERALDS the beginning of nightly preshow routines for company members, starting with fight call at 5:45 in the afternoon.

As Robert Midgette, fight director, and Philip Culton, fight captain, begin their run-through of the fight scenes, I can hear the other preshow rituals happening offstage. The choir is warming up by the costume shop, their voices rising and falling toward the setting sun. Undoubtedly, the dancers are quietly congregating and stretching in the sound stage. The electricians have materialized, too.

The electricians have one of the most bizarre preshow duties to perform. Today, Elton Bradley, one of the follow spot operators, has drawn the short straw. Wearing his rigging harness, he ascends one of the two massive light towers sprouting from the decorative turrets that flank the sides of the theater, to the top platform where the lighting instruments hang.

"Heads up!" he yells. "Sticks coming down!"

Bradley kicks off half a dozen tree limbs. They are not as thick as my wrist, but some are about two feet long. As the tops of the towers are far above the tops of the trees, there is only one way they could have gotten there.

"Ospreys?" I ask Sydney Norris, the electrics crew chief standing near me. She nods.

"How often do they try to build nests up there?"

"Practically every day," she says. "But this is a national park, which means that if they succeeded in building a completed nest, we would have to leave it. If they were an endangered species, we'd have to let them build nests. But they're on least-threatened status, so we can kick the sticks off before they build a fire hazard."

"Are they aggressive?" I ask. "Are they territorial?"

"Very."

Painting up every night is a messy business. Left to right: Colin Tripp, Matt Gabbard, Vitally Mayes, Philip Culton. Photo by Matt Gabbard

Even after opening night, the show might have rough edges to be polished in brush-up rehearsals, but if the show is running smoothly the rehearsals and classes and work calls will be held only for a few hours once a week, giving the company members time to catch their breath. On a practical level, this means there is enough time to drive into Manteo and launder the dirty clothes that have piled up during the past weeks.

Tending to the clothes worn onstage falls to the costumers, of course, who clean costumes in accordance with a rotating schedule. One young woman carries hangers of "good colonist" costumes with both hands, two hats sitting precariously on her head. Another carries four-foot-wide farthingales, one in each hand, held high so as not to touch the ground. Still another wheels a twenty-gallon electric air compressor. Mehron-brand liquid makeup will be airbrushed onto actors inside an eight-by-eight-foot spray booth, darkening the skin of those who portray the Native Americans, and hand-painted designs replicating John White's drawings will be added by the wardrobe stitchers after the base paint dries. That makeup stains the costumes, and backstage benches are dedicated specifically for those wearing body paint. The benches are easy to spot; just look for red butt prints.

Actors arrive in groups according to their call times. They sign in at the backstage company call board, some of them dropping off their bags and packs

*O*ne summer during the scene between the Runner and John Borden, the crowd was gathering around onstage as John gave his lines, then the guy playing the Runner says out loud, "Friends, a Roman ship is anchored at the bar!" Now, everyone was ready to do their reactions about the Spanish ship; instead, many began to pretend to cry, to cover the fact they were about to die laughing. I was standing next to John Borden. I looked at him and under my breath whispered, "Et tu, John Borden?" Borden turned and walked into the Chapel with his back to the audience so no one would see him laughing. It took a couple of moments, but everyone pulled themselves together and finished the scene. Much laughter in the dressing rooms afterward!

—— MICHAEL CAMPBELL
(1985–90, 1992–94, 1996–97, 2004, 2009–10, 2014)

and water bottles in the dressing rooms before heading to the mainstage if they have fight call.

In a larger sense, opening night fixes life for the next three months. The company performs six nights a week, and their days will be largely their own. The frantic pace of rehearsals slackens abruptly. With that glut of free time, the shimmering vision of a summer at the beach finally opens like a broad vista viewed from a magic carpet ride.

Because they are aspiring young professionals, many cast and crew members throw themselves into the shows produced by *The Lost Colony*'s

Relaxing backstage. Photo by Ira David Wood III

Emily Asbury makes productive use of her time as she waits backstage for her scene as Queen Elizabeth I. Photo by Jamil Zraikat

Professional Theatre Workshop. Some get day jobs waiting tables or operating cash registers or taking tickets at one of the businesses that serve the legions of tourists who troop to the Outer Banks. A few do very little, preferring to sleep in their air-conditioned apartments all day with the blinds shut tight. Some are all about spending their days on the beach and road-tripping or camping on their day off. Still others stay up all night every night just to see the sun rise.

One way or another, everyone is on their own individual journey, so everyone gets locked into their own groove like a needle on a record, the needle centered in the rhythms of the call times and spinning to the speed of the calendar page, a groove seventy-five shows long, a private, personal groove driven by the big show that lasts all summer. That record plays their song, the song of themselves, for the first time because most of these young artists have never had an extended run like this. Most are straight out of school, where their shows ran for a week or a weekend. A months-long run is a foreign experience, and they react in different ways, since it takes hard work to keep the experience exciting to both themselves and the audience. They will learn that often the only way to keep it fresh is by choosing which shoe to put on first. On Monday, begin with the left foot; on Tuesday, start with the right. Consciously practicing these tiny variations in nightly routines is the best way to keep from wilting in the heat.

Charity Sellers adjusts John Bennett's Wingina costume. Photo by Jamil Zraikat

This Is Where I Scream at You

Since Robert Midgette became fight director in 2006, he has employed technology and special effects to give audiences more of what they love: big, dramatic, cinematic fight scenes.

ALL ACTORS EVEN PERIPHERALLY INVOLVED in stage combat rehearse their sequences before every show to keep fight choreography fresh in their minds for safety. The fight captain, Philip Culton, works the necessary replacement actors into the individual sequences, called "tracks." Tonight, for example, Old Tom's understudy is going on; the actor normally playing the role has had a death in the family, and not only must the understudy rehearse the track, but since he is usually an AT involved in the Big Battle, Philip must assign another actor to cover the understudy's track, too. Domino effects like this ripple through every aspect of the show. It should come as no surprise that the first words from stage management at the beginning of every night's show are, "Here are tonight's replacements."

"Happy Monday, guys," says Philip to the actors sitting down front in the shaded seats of the house. "I have one note from the last show: please don't stand around the gun case. It slows the people who need to get or return a gun in a hurry. Thanks. Let's run tracks."

Philip works with the understudy and his replacement. Several other actors join them onstage in the sand, and the little committee assigns business. They decide who can strike King Wingina's war club, who has time to put out one actor's torch, who is near enough to join the bucket brigade putting out the structure fire in the Big Battle. All these individual pieces of business are necessary to keep the action flowing smoothly and, above all, safely. Breaking fight choreography can have ruinous consequences.

"Let's run Big Battle," Philip says, and the actors not already onstage get up from the house with general enthusiasm, clapping their hands and whooping it up. In no time, everyone is standing in the sand on the mainstage, and the disjointed clapping morphs into the rhythmic clapping at the beginning of the song "Car Wash" by Rose Royce.

Jake Newcomb in the sound booth cues the music for the battle, and as the war drums start, general screaming announces the Indian attack onstage. The actors rehearse without the intensity of the live show, marking most of the action. Most of the dead and dying do not lie down but stand in place. Standing dead men yawn and stretch and scratch their beards; resurrection is part of their daily fare.

"This is where I scream at you," says an actress in shorts to an actor with a Mohawk.

"I'm okay with that," he replies.

During the battle, an actress accidentally kicks sand all over an actor playing dead downstage right. She gasps at her carelessness, but since the action is happening center, she tiptoes downstage to him, where she kneels and gently brushes the sand off the actor's face and out of his eyes.

The Big Battle rehearsal ends, followed by a few quick questions and answers as other actors move on to the Plymouth fight between John Borden and Simon Fernando. The actors know the track by now and mark it professionally. Even Philip says, "Let's not get too sandy too soon," as they move on to the Ralph Lane scene.

With more than two and a half hours to go before show time, pyrotechnician Stephen Turner is already hard at work loading and testing one of the five fog machines deployed during the show.

"I tried coming in with everyone else my first year," he says as he gooses the black box with fog juice. "We were all over each other, so I come in early."

He must prep for the "Burning Girl," a staged pyrotechnical stunt involving an actress running in a flaming dress. There are several staged structural fires fueled by propane tanks, which must be inspected and tested. And those guns

Philip Culton played the role of Wanchese in the 2017 season and served as fight captain, supporting the fight director. Photo by Jamil Zraikat

Fight director Robert Midgette has heightened the excitement of the battle scenes by introducing more and bigger special effects, including a more dramatic portrayal of the Burning Girl. Photo courtesy of *The Lost Colony*

will not clean and load themselves. There are also more than a dozen torches. Eleven of these are battle torches, meaning their handles are dressed metal pipe that will not break during stage combat. Stephen is a busy man; I have yet to see him sitting down.

"Yeah, I need to get in early, especially before AT setup," he continues, peering into one of the many white five-gallon buckets of sand backstage. These buckets extinguish the torches and must be inspected for loose combustibles from the previous show.

With the tracks run, Robert Midgette and Philip Culton compliment everyone on their hard work and remind them to keep up their intensity. Everyone has just enjoyed a day off, and Monday shows are typically the least energetic for that reason. That said, they move on to the Ralph Lane fight,

where Robert times actor entrances and exits to prevent them from bunching up on the side stage.

"Yeah, my bad," says one actor, referring to a late entrance the previous show.

"But you know about it?" asks Robert, not as an accusation but simply to know if the actor is aware of the missed cue. "Okay. Then let's run it."

The actors run their tracks, and Robert coaches them to step back from the scene, which feels counterintuitive but which utilizes the natural scenery so that the audience's eye will see the individual tracks.

"Open up. Give them the space. Play this way, instead of that way," he says as he adjusts one actor's blocking. "Better. Play it back, not forward."

He has been with *The Lost Colony* for forty-three years, twenty-six in

The Big Battle scene features fifteen torches and more than twenty gunshots. Photo by Delena Gray Ostrander

Robert Midgette has been with *The Lost Colony* for more than forty years, 26 in the principal role of Manteo. He is pictured here with Brian Wescott in the role of Manteo's son. Photo courtesy of *The Lost Colony*

Onstage foes, offstage friends: Pete Peterson (left) and Robert Midgette worked together as Wanchese and Manteo for 18 years. Photo courtesy of *The Lost Colony*

the principal role of Manteo, a record that remains unchallenged for any role. Since Robert Midgette became fight director in 2006, he has employed technology and special effects to give audiences more of what they love: big, dramatic, cinematic fight scenes.

"When I first played the role of Manteo, we only had three torches and maybe five gunshots in the whole show," says Robert. "Since then, we've added about fifteen torches, probably twenty live gunshots, and made the 'Burning Girl' a much bigger effect. Plus, we have a great sound designer, Michael Rasbury, and surround-sound capabilities, which make for a more dramatic scene."

Robert draws from his vast experience with different directors to design the fight scenes. "Joe Layton used to say that because the stage is so big, you have to think of it like the audience is watching a movie. So, during the battle scenes, instead of having all the action happen at one time all over the place,

*T*his was in 1996, the last day of the season, and the last year Pete Peterson played Wanchese. Pete and I had worked together for eighteen years. Back then, we didn't have a daily fight call like we do today, so the principal actors didn't have to report until 7:45 P.M. When I arrived, someone told me, "Pete's real sick, and we don't know if he can do the show." I went to the nurse's shack to see him, and sure enough he had a bad case of food poisoning. The problem was, his understudy had left a week early, so we had no understudy for his part. The only thing we could do was to have my understudy go on in my role as Manteo, and for me to play Wanchese, which I had never done before. That means I had to do the paint design for Wanchese, all the lines, and his side of the fight scenes. I had to reverse everything without rehearsing any of it. Of all the shows I ever did, that was probably the most interesting. It was mentally exhausting, but we got through it. I still remember the feeling of relief.

—— ROBERT MIDGETTE (1961–)

Waiting to cause mayhem in the Big Battle scene. Photo by Kieron Cotter

I try to imagine it like a movie camera, so the audience can follow it with their eyes."

From director Fred Chappell, he learned to slow the action to help the audience focus. "Movements have to be big, bold, and deliberate, and just underneath natural speed," he says.

"David Wood has a unique perspective because he's done the show as a performer, which very few directors have. He understands what it's like to work in extreme conditions—heat, cold, wind. Even during auditions, he tells people exactly what they can expect. You have to be prepared for the conditions physically and with your voice. It takes real endurance to finish the season and stay healthy."

When Robert and Philip finish the run-through, a single-engine plane buzzes overhead on the flight path to the Manteo airport, calling our attention to the towering clouds in the southern sky. As the drone of the engine fades away, Robert turns to me and says, "Eleven hundred in advance ticket sales for tonight. We better not have a rainout."

Rising from the Ashes

THE CREATORS OF *The Lost Colony* never expected it to last more than one season, yet in its original form the show ran during the summer months for an incredible four years, until blackout restrictions shut down Waterside Theatre for the duration of World War II. Even before war was officially declared, wreckage and oil slicks from Nazi U-boat attacks washed up on the beaches of the Outer Banks.

When performances of *The Lost Colony* resumed in the summer of 1946, the spirit and timbre of the show changed. The war had wrought vast, inestimable changes on America, and the Outer Banks had lost its share of citizens in combat. And three founding members of the show's producing company, the Roanoke Island Historical Association, were dead.

D. B. Fearing, W. O. Saunders, and Proff Koch had been driving forces in the original production. Fearing was the dynamic civic leader who extended electrical lines from the town of Manteo to power the lights and sound. When he died in 1943, fifty uniformed airmen were posted as his honor guard. Saunders was the crusading journalist who from his offices at the *Elizabeth City Independent* agitated for the creation of the show and served as its public relations man. In 1940, his car swerved off the road late one night, and he disappeared into the Great Dismal Swamp Canal. Proff Koch, from whose Carolina Playmakers playwright Paul Green had sprung as if fully formed, died of a heart attack in 1944. All three were tireless boosters for the show and the Outer Banks.

"Those men were larger than life," says Paul Green Jr., who lived with the Fearing family in Manteo during the summer of 1941 while working as an electrician in the show. He remembers well the efforts of his father and

When The Lost Colony resumed performances in the summer of 1946, the spirit and timbre of the show changed.

When fire destroyed much of Waterside Theatre in 1947, its original architect, Skipper Bell, led the community to accomplish the rebuild in just six days. Photo courtesy of *The Lost Colony*

the native islanders to promote both the show and the Outer Banks as a destination.

"To get to Manteo, we drove to Elizabeth City," he tells me over lunch. "We recited the play to each other word for word on the drive down. There was no road at all below Whalebone; it was just sand. There was nothing down there all the way to Hatteras.

"They were just in time," he continues after a bite from his sandwich. "*The Lost Colony* brought the tourists, and the tourists brought development. They were in the right time together. They had a symbiosis." Then he adds thoughtfully, "I think I know why it's lasted. It's a good play. I think it's my father's best."

But the terrible fire at Waterside Theatre in July 1947 most directly necessitated the postwar changes in the show.

No one knows how the fire started, but at 4:40 P.M. a watchman discovered it and called the fire department. Fanned by strong winds, the fire jumped from the scene dock to the choir loft to the Organ House to the mainstage, and then it jumped to the dressing rooms, igniting a tunnel of fire that burned furiously down the hallway dividing the two open halves that were a peculiar feature of that structure. The mainstage burned. The shop burned. The fire burned out of control for almost ninety minutes, consuming props, scenery, tools, stocked material and supplies, and every page of recorded *Lost Colony* history stored there.

Armed with nothing but a ring of keys, Irene Smart (Rains) saved the costumes. She and nearby residents unlocked dressing rooms and advanced inside to grab what costumes they could and carry them out of the building by the armful. Their quick thinking and prompt action saved immeasurable effort and cost in reconstruction; if the costumes had burned, the season would have ended on July 24, simply because there would not have been enough time to rebuild the hundreds of individual pieces necessary. Miss Rene and her crew created the chance to save the season, and Waterside Theatre architect Skipper Bell rose to that challenge.

"I remember Skipper Bell hauling away the burned lumber before it even cooled," says Marjalene Thomas. "He was pulling timbers out by hand and rolling them away. I remember the smoking ends bouncing. He was pulling still-burning wood out of the piles."

The work of the Manteo Fire Department's pump trucks paid off. By six o'clock, the fire was declared under control. A meeting was called on the still-smoking apron down front. By this time, nearly the entire cast and crew were at the theater, and everyone present pledged to do whatever had to be done to rebuild immediately.

"Give me some lumber and some men and I will rebuild the theater in four or five days," announced Skipper Bell.

In a meeting at the Dare County Courthouse, citizens offered not only lumber and nails but tools and trained hands to wield them. The whole town of Manteo, if not the entire island, was mobilized by eight-thirty that night, and the trucks began rolling to and from the ruins of Waterside Theatre. Local handymen built props in private backyard shops while journeymen carpenters constructed scenery inside an empty hangar at the airport. At the theater, untrained men with axes and adzes and drawknives chopped and notched

> *"Give me some lumber and some men and I will rebuild the theater in four or five days," announced Skipper Bell.*

I witnessed the whole thing from the side stage. Andy Griffith was Sir Walter Raleigh that year, and one night the actress who played Queen Elizabeth was so drunk she couldn't remember her lines. It was the Queen's Garden scene. Andy would say his lines and then, fast, feed her lines to her, and she would garble them. I don't know how he kept a straight face. Finally, the stage managers came to the realization that she could not do the whole show. They got Mary Long, her understudy, ready to go on. Mary was half the size of the queen, and there was only one queen's costume that fit her, but they got her in it. When the queen came offstage, someone clamped a hand over her mouth. There was someone to grab each arm and each leg, and they swooped her up and away so she couldn't make a commotion. The only thing they needed from her was the wig. They got it all done just in time for Mary to go on and say, "La, what a wrecking of times when a queen must chase after a man!" You could hear a murmur go through the audience because of course the only thing that was the same about the queen was the wig. I heard Andy tell that story so many times. He would dramatize it just as it happened. It was a joy to watch.

— EDDIE GREENE (1953–54)

pine logs while experienced journeymen laid flooring and erected walls. By all accounts, Skipper Bell's leadership was inspiring. Work went on twenty-four hours a day.

In six days, they had their miracle. There were lots of loose ends, to be sure: scenery missing hardware; electrical fixtures in the makeup room without wiring; incomplete reed thatching on roofs; the Chapel and one of the cabins still under construction. But these minor details only highlighted the scale of what those exhausted, dirty, sweaty people accomplished. When the lights went up, the company played their hearts out as they had never done before.

One of those company members was a first-year actor and former music major from the University of North Carolina in Chapel Hill. His wife, Barbara, who had played Eleanor Dare, talked him into coming to Manteo to be in *The Lost Colony*, and he landed the role of First Soldier. His name was Andrew Griffith.

Andrew and Barbara returned in 1948, she to play Eleanor while he donned the armor again, this time to play the Second Soldier. He later said he hated wearing the steel armor and dreaded the sound of thunder, for he was sure he would be struck by lightning. While armor is still worn in the show, both the First and Second Soldiers have been cut from the current production.

From 1949 until 1953, Andrew played Sir Walter Raleigh and Barbara played Eleanor Dare. For extra money, they performed with other colonists in late-night floor shows at the old Shriners Club on the beach in Nags Head. Barbara danced, and Andrew posed as a bumpkin preacher who told jokes and related comic anecdotes in brief monologues. They were dirt poor.

"I remember them backstage," says Della Basnight, who was a colonist kid in the show back then. "Barbara would pause at the window of the men's dressing room, hold out her hand, and say, 'Andrew, give me the dime.' Then Sir Walter's arm would come through the window and give her their one dime so she could go buy a big fountain drink at the concession stand for them to split."

Griffith honed his monologues. By 1953, he was performing his routines on the local convention circuit, including one called, "What It Was, Was Football," which he recorded. Five hundred copies were pressed, and it became a hit on regional radio. Capitol Records scooped him up, and by 1955 he was on Broadway in the comedy *No Time for Sergeants*. It ran for two years.

Pirates on the North Pole

These people have been working hard for almost five weeks, and they show it.

IT IS TEN O'CLOCK on this bright and breezy Saturday morning in early June, and *The Lost Colony* children's show is rehearsing in the sound stage. The sash windows wrapping the three sound sides of the building are open, and a cool, moist breeze blows right off the water, making the black masking curtains sway. The actors are performing with their backs to the sound, and a blinding glare from the bright light outside the open windows obscures their faces.

The children's show is the first show produced by the Professional Theater Workshop (PTW). Typically, it showcases some of the most talented members of the company who do not perform leading roles in the big show. The director, too, is usually up and coming, and PTW credits look good on résumés in the fall; it shows you came here to work, not lie on the beach all day. That you performed your part well or directed with style is implied, if for no other reason than that you beat out the other company members to be in this, the premier production.

The show this year is a funny piece of musical fantasy entitled *Jingle ARRGH the Way*, book, music, and lyrics by Janet Yates Vogt and Mark Friedman, the premise being that a pirate ship goes to the North Pole and meets Santa. It offers singing and dancing and piratical dialogue spiced with jokes, some of which only the parents will get. It should be a winner, and it will run for almost two months, which also reads well on a résumé; most college shows close after a week or two, and an extended run teaches young actors discipline.

"You'll have the mirror today," says director Kole McKinley as he gestures toward the two large rolling mirrors. "You won't have it on Monday. Use it to check your spacing. Places for the top of the run. Sarah will be on book." The taped music starts, but almost immediately there is a botched sound cue, followed by, "Hold, please," from the sound op.

"Good heavens," says Jordan Prescott, music director for the show. He sits out front.

"I see someone didn't get their eight hours of sleep last night," says a cast member toward the sound table. Sleep in the Grove can be problematic, but while these people appear tired, looks can be deceiving. I know Kole has gone on in his understudy role in the main production twice already, and will go on again tonight. These people have been working hard for almost five weeks, and they show it.

Every summer, some of *The Lost Colony*'s most promising young actors participate in shows staged by the Professional Theater Workshop as an opportunity to gain experience and hone their skills. In 2017, PTW presented a children's show, *Jingle ARRGH the Way*. Left to right: Landon Scott Ferrell as Santa, Vitally Mayes, Delphon Curtis Jr. as Braidbeard, Colin Tripp, Megan Glover. Photo courtesy of *The Lost Colony*

The music starts again, and the rehearsal lurches forward. The actors mime most of the props, which have not yet been built, and for the most part they are off book. The action moves forward in fits and starts, but when they say, "Line," they generally are not breaking character. It is truly a stumble-through, not a run-through, and when the actors blank the action grinds to a halt.

But one musical number catches me off guard: a jazzy piece with a high-hat cymbal hissing and lots of finger snapping, as between the Sharks and the Jets in *West Side Story*. In a rehearsed burst of spontaneity, Caitlyn Leach, who plays the gourmet pirate Pierre, launches into a tap dance. She is really selling it, too, hoofing all over the stage while Kole shows a sight gag to another pirate who is steering the removable ship's wheel.

One actor has not been onstage at all, sitting quietly in a chair off to one side. When I go to him and ask who he plays, he says, "I'm Santa. I'll go on as soon as they reach the North Pole." Then he adds, "It's very soon."

The pirates are navigating the Arctic now, and when they see a polar bear the sound op hits the cue. A basso profundo voice says, "I love you."

Everyone stops dead and starts laughing. As the sound op is looking through her notes, she says, "It's on the track provided!" and everyone laughs harder.

Hardship, Weal, and Woe

A LOGJAM IS HAPPENING on the mainstage during preshow setup, and the work center stage stops. Until an AT monkeys up to the top of the Chapel roof to clear a fouled guideline hung in one of the pulleys, the monster flat will not fly. While the AT makes his way gingerly over the cypress shakes of the steeply pitched roof, the usually smooth routine onstage abruptly slows then stops in the hot afternoon. Shirtless young men and young women in sports bras, all of them wearing shorts, simply stop in midstep, waiting for the all clear. As the minutes tick by, the monster flats slowly sink into the sand one by one, lowered there by their panting handlers.

And hot it is; all three of the weather apps I have on my phone say it is somewhere between ninety-one and ninety-six degrees, and with the humidity the heat index is over one hundred. They ought to just call it the misery

Actors in *The Lost Colony* take their rest where they can find it. Photo courtesy of *The Lost Colony*

index at this point because direct sunlight also pours through the stage-right wing onto anyone standing in the sand.

Two female ATs in sunglasses appear from the sunlit stage-right wing carrying the large platform for the throne in the Queen's Garden scene, the one in front walking backward as the other guides her. Suddenly made aware of the problem onstage, they stop in their tracks to become part of the traffic jam. Heavy platform still in hand, they stand still for a minute in the hot sun, sweat streaming off their bodies.

"It's too hot for this," says one of the female ATs, and they set down the platform in the sand to wait for the problem to be fixed.

"I believe in you, Carey," says electrician Jesse Byron from the shade of the house. She pulls down her Jackie O shades to the tip of her nose and winks elaborately at him.

AT Christopher Keil tries to keep cool backstage. Photo by Jamil Zraikat

After Johnny Underwood straightens out the problem, talking the rooftop AT through the necessary steps, the progression of scenery resumes. In the stage-left wing, two male ATs slide a parapet flat out of the scene dock, lifting it clear and turning in one motion to approach the stairs. But they have started their tilt too soon, and the top of the flat crashes against the framing of the scene dock, the lumber and plywood scraping against each other until the monster clears the dock, gliding silently away like the *Titanic* past the iceberg that sank her.

Looking at the flat as they pass me, I see raw wood where the collision occurred, but the condition of the top of the flat indicates this has happened before, probably many times. The plywood is chewed to splinters, and the original shape is battered beyond recognition; still, that will not appear to the audience seated fifty feet away. It is best merely to touch it up with paint as needed on a weekly basis, since there is no structural damage.

"Is this the day it breaks?" says one AT to the other as they turn to rush up the parapet steps.

"I swear it's like playing Russian roulette," grunts the other as they surge up

They ought to call it the misery index because direct sunlight also pours through the stage-right wing onto anyone standing in the sand.

the stairs. Now that I am looking up at the back of the flat, I see a prominent mending plate on a break in the framing.

Two ATs walk by with the big totem pole; two others join them, and with Johnny they raise it, Iwo Jima style, until it drops into its sleeved hole. The big totem is an aluminum tube with arms TIG welded in place, then scenically dressed. The ATs place the other totems, which are extruded foam covered in burlap. A couple of ATs place the baskets of plastic corn and squash nearby, and about half a dozen start raking the sand.

"Someone busted their butt over here," says an AT with a rake on the Indian Stage. Apparently, someone went flying in last night's Big Battle; a huge skid mark stretches from one end of the stage to the other.

Johnny Underwood sprays water from a large garden hose over the sand to keep the dust down during the Indian Dance.

On the grass of the apron, AT Jonathan Varillas leans on a rake, sweating and panting. "Johnny, it's hot!" he complains loudly, as if Johnny can do something about the weather.

"Oh yeah? Ya think so, Jonathan?" he says, and then turns and sprays him with the hose until he screams.

ATs often play multiple roles onstage. For example, in 2017, Kelsea Tyler, shown here in makeup for his role as the Dead Body, also played a Colonist, the Sailor who rides the ship's mast at the end of Act I, and the Queen's Messenger. Photo by Jamil Zraikat

I think my worst memory of performing in *The Lost Colony* had to be one that involved buttcans. Buttcans, the large, old coffee cans painted red that hung on a nail on the offstage wall next to every stage entrance. Buttcans, where smokers like myself (I smoked a lot back in the mid-eighties but quit in the mid-nineties) could drop their cigarette butts before going onstage. Buttcans, filled with water and, over a few days' time, dozens of cigarette butts. One fateful night, I was making an entrance through the upstage-right doorway. I wasn't even smoking at that moment. Maybe it was fate. Maybe it was a sign. But it definitely was a mess. As I stepped through the doorway, my right shoulder hit the bottom of the buttcan in question. Quickly, silently, it fell from its nail, dumping its damp, sodden, smelly contents all over me and my costume. Next thing I know, I'm onstage in the middle of a crowd scene. As the scene continued, cast members around me began to move away from me ever so slowly on all sides, leaving me alone in an empty circle. Even my cast "wife" and "child" abandoned me. Worst of all was the look on Queen Elizabeth's face as the crowd parted and she walked past me. Sorry, Your Majesty, I thought to myself. That damned Virginia tobacco will get you every time.

— GEORGE JACK (1985, 1987–88)

Keepers of a Dream

This show could not ask for a more raucous bunch of boosters.

THEY COME FROM ALL OVER the country, like Darrin Larson from Dallas and Doc Winstead from Florida and Mark Cantrell from West Virginia. They also come from just up the road, like Gail Hutchison and David Miller and Hunt Thomas. They are the former cast and crew members of *The Lost Colony* attending the alumni reunion that has been planned to mark the eightieth season, and I am one of them.

On a sultry Friday evening at the end of June, more than a hundred of us are gathering inside one of the large, air-conditioned halls of Roanoke Island Festival Park in Manteo. The stooped and the aged are here with motorized chairs and walkers and canes, even ski poles for assistance, but this show could not ask for a more raucous bunch of boosters.

Some of these people worked the show before Morrison Grove existed. They found lodging at the private residences of families with names such as Twiford and Owens and Evans. Some of these homes are now the finest B&Bs on the island.

A lot of colonists bunked together in rented houses denoted by the names of their owners, such as the Pennystone House, or places with nicknames such as "the Tepee" and "the Wigwam," buildings torn down decades ago. Eddie Greene, a dancer in 1954 and one of the oldest alumni present, rented a house with no windows or doors his first summer. Local kids came to gawk at the beaded curtain he used for a front door; it was the first they had ever seen.

Yes, some of us move more slowly now, but our eyes shine and our voices ring when we see old friends and remember our shows. And if the young, inexperienced colonists performing tonight's show on the north end of the island are green, then we are gray.

In 2017, alumni joined with the current cast and crew to celebrate *The Lost Colony*'s eightieth season. Photo by Delena Gray Ostrander

Looking around the packed, noisy room, it appears that red-headed Zeb Hults is the only person here without at least a touch of gray hair, but this is probably just a trick of the fading light. Zeb is taller than I remember, so his healthy head of hair makes him easy to spot. After our first handshake in more than a decade, he introduces Elizabeth and me to his fiancée, an orchestra conductor. Elizabeth jokes with her about the burden she will assume when she marries an alumnus, introducing her to the term "*Colony*-in-law."

"We'll form a support group," I hear Elizabeth say as I go toward the bar to get her a glass of wine.

But I cannot take three steps without looking into the faces of old friends. Here by a round table stands Mike Campbell laughing with Jerry Vess. When we three toured with the Patchwork Players in the off-season, I never laughed so hard in my life. Over there is Aaron Cooke, a fellow AT from years ago. Aaron was "the Rock of the Dock," meaning scene dock; he made me feel safe

*I*t was 1981, my first summer at *The Lost Colony*. A bunch of us were at Coquina Beach. As I was swimming in the water, I saw a couple of people laughing up a storm. I floated over to them and introduced myself. They were Haskell Fitz-Simmons and Maggie. "Here, hold our beers," said Haskell. So I did. They both dove under the water and came back up with their swimsuits over their heads, like nun habits! They then commenced to sing, "How do you solve a problem like Maria?" in perfect tune with each other. Haskell then looked at me and said, "How do you like dat?" And that's how I learned to become a sea nun. I was hooked! Haskell and I became the best of friends. When he took his final march, I told that story at his memorial service.

— GAIL HUTCHISON (1981–83, 1985, 1988–92)

The principal players from the 1990 season in an often-used image affectionately called "Family Portrait" by alumni. Front row, left to right: Joshua Livesay as Wano, Robert Midgette as Manteo, Stacey Maxwell as Manteo's wife, Barbara Hird as Queen Elizabeth I, Hank Hale as Simon Fernando, Gail Hutchison as Agona. Back row, left to right: Britt Solano as John Borden, Frank Roberts as Sir Walter Raleigh, Terrence McCrossan as Ananias Dare, Madeline Rains as Eleanor Dare, Bryan Jones as Governor White, Pete Peterson as Wanchese, Pat Hurley as Old Tom. Photo by Walter V. Gresham III, courtesy of *The Lost Colony*

when we humped that scenery together, and even tonight he looks as strong as ever. Aaron is a photographer living in Clemson, South Carolina, and says he decided at the last minute to jump in his car and drive to the reunion. There sits Pat Hurley, a former Old Tom who now teaches aspiring actors in Atlanta. Over there is Charles Winstead, or "Charlie Tuna," one of my ATs from 1998. The three Furr girls are here, too, and so is Cynthia Furr Linton, their mother. Susan and Robin Knowles are here also, husbands in tow.

"This is no place for an introvert," says Katelan Simon, now Kate Cobb, when I bump into her. Kate and I toured together in the fall of 1987 after leaving Roanoke Island. "I'm completely overwhelmed."

"I am, too, and I'm not an introvert."

Thirty-four years of my life appear in front of me, but out of sequence and compressed, stretching the laws of space and time, warping reality. Faces and voices from my distant past are suddenly only an arm's length away. All I have to do is reach out to touch them.

There are Mike and Nina Repeta, a couple I have not seen in thirty years. Mike is a film guy now, a cameraman based out of Wilmington. Nina, a

After performing in *The Lost Colony*, Terrence Mann went on to a successful career in theater, including the role of Rum Tum Tugger in the Broadway production of Cats. He returned to direct *The Lost Colony* for two years. Photo courtesy of *The Lost Colony*

working actress, played Bessie Potter on *Dawson's Creek* for years when that show filmed in Wilmington. Mike laughs when I ask how they got their start at the *Colony*.

"We were in school together at East Carolina University when I got cast in the show as an AT. I said to Nina, 'You're the one with talent. You should be doing the show, too,' and she got hired as a dancer."

Nearby stand another pair of ECU graduates: Chris and Marilyn Chappell. Marilyn, a former dancer with the show, owns and operates a dance studio in Holly Springs. Chris also danced in the show and was the most athletic John Borden I ever saw. Chris, about to retire from teaching drama in the North Carolina public school system, talks about how he came to be with *The Lost Colony*. "I was taking dance classes in Greenville," says Chris. "Mavis Ray was my dance teacher, and she said, 'You're going to Manteo this summer.' I didn't even know where Manteo was."

At a table by the windows are former colonists Clark and Melissa Nicholson, founders of the Gamut Theatre Group in Harrisburg, Pennsylvania. Their creations include the Harrisburg Shakespeare Company and a children's theater company, the Popcorn Hat Players. I ask Clark to remind me how he got cast.

"I was with you! Remember?" he says. "We drove to locals in the winter of '88."

After dark, Elizabeth and I walk in the warm night air back to the Roanoke Island Inn. In the comfort of the air-conditioned room, as we crawl between the clean white sheets, I casually ask her if she had a good time tonight.

"They're the most engaging people I've ever met," she says as she turns off the light.

*D*uring rehearsals, another cast member and I stopped in at the Subway in Manteo. As we were ordering, in walks Terrence Mann. He invited us to eat lunch with him. He was so down-to-earth and personable. We talked about music and normal everyday stuff. Interacting with him as a person and not just a director was truly unforgettable. Being in *The Lost Colony*, first as a child actor and then as a member of the choir, was an experience like no other. We had the opportunity to learn from professionals such as Jacques d'Amboise, Frank Wildhorn, and Ann Reinking in workshops. Nowhere else in the world can you learn from the best in the business, have a sandwich with your Broadway idol, and then perform nightly with future Broadway stars, all against the backdrop of the most beautiful sunset in the United States. I hope people will continue to carry the legacy on for many generations to come.

— ASHLEY PHILLIPS WHITE (1996, 2001)

A Mug of Plymouth Ale

Parties in Morrison Grove are the stuff of legend, and their names say it all.

"A LITTLE TO YOUR RIGHT," says Sir Walter Raleigh to the driver of the old pickup truck. The young, bearded driver, his head sticking out the window to get a better backward view, spins the steering wheel with one arm before he continues backing up the narrow asphalt path from the parking lot toward the center of Morrison Grove. Sir Walter wears a Hawaiian shirt and shorts, as tonight's performance ended an hour ago, and on Saturday night that means it is party time in the Grove.

"Straight back, my Fordly friend!" he continues as the truck squeezes past the stairs leading to one of the apartment buildings.

"Did I clear the railing?" yells the driver over the sound of the motor.

"Straight back, O great long-bedded one!" He is enjoying himself immensely.

The truck clears the steps and the railing to reach the open, flat ground of the common area. Here, it stops and clanks into drive. He turns to his left and pulls ahead, nosing the reeking vehicle forward until it almost touches another building, where he parks and kills the engine. The whole Grove smells like gasoline.

A gang of young men swarm over the truck. Several break out a folded blue tarp and quickly, expertly, almost professionally spread it inside the bed with its edges lapping the sides. Pairs of men appear out of the darkness lugging great tubs of ice between them, tubs they empty into the back of the truck. Then, in unison, they go to the nearby grill table, pulling out cases of beer from underneath, shredding the cardboard with their bare hands, and dumping the cans of beer in one quick motion into the back of the truck. I find myself sucked in, pulled along, helping out, just another guy on the Mo' Grove prefab party crew. I stop counting the cases.

Old Tom's (Robert Hooghkirk) fondness for Plymouth ale gets him in trouble with the Landlord (Christopher Charleston). Photo by Delena Gray Ostrander

Brandon Cheney tends the grill, never moving, focused on making little pizzas. Out of the darkness, cornhole boards and beer pong tables appear, as if someone threw a switch. On cue, a guitar amplifier begins blasting dance music.

"Are we ready?" asks Jake Johnson, a dancer.

General nods and affirmatives quickly follow from the prefab party crew. As one, they crack open their cans of beer, hold them in the air, and yell at the top of their lungs, "*Chirp!*"

I wonder about the etymology of this tradition. The only thing I can imagine is that some sober authority figure must have once reprimanded the

Good clean fun aside, they are young and indestructible; fueled by cheap beer and spaghetti, they will run all summer.

company members for the noise, saying he wanted to hear only crickets coming from Morrison Grove.

Good luck with that, because the parties in Morrison Grove are the stuff of legend, and their names say it all: Name Tag, Christmas in July, Trailer Trash, Prom, Polyester, Dead Celebrity, Come As You're Not, Frothy Drink, Noah's Ark (where not only are you furry, but you have to come two by two), Mai Tai/Tie Dye, Tie and Underwear. One year, some guys even threw a Better Dwayne Than Me party.

Good clean fun aside, the participants are young and indestructible; fueled by cheap beer and spaghetti, they will run all summer. Things get wild, but since they know they all must go to work together the day after the party, things rarely get ugly. They are also young enough not to know personal or professional failure, so they are incredibly optimistic, and this makes them try dangerous things, such as taking a kayak and trying to row to Croatoan—Hatteras Island—not because no one has tried it before, and not because they are bored, but because it is specifically they who have not tried to do it. And since they are indestructible, they could be the first person to circumnavigate Roanoke Island in an inflatable beach float.

Unfortunately, this usually means a swamped canoe or a deflated raft, and someone such as Robert Midgette, who owns a powerboat, must pull them out of the water or out of the reeds in Manns Harbor. So beware, for those whom the gods would destroy, they first call "talented."

One of my favorite memories of a summer filled with delightful experiences is arriving at Crab Carnage with Carina Day (now Dacierno). Indulging my fondness for *Gilligan's Island*, she agreed to sit in an inflatable boat dressed as Lovey Howell, while I, in full Thurston Howell III regalia, rowed us around a small peninsula and onto the beach. (We liked grand entrances, okay?) All went well for a few minutes, but the oars were ungainly and kept bumping the champagne bucket (we went full-out Howell on this thing), and it soon became obvious that ditching the oars and having Thurston pull Lovey ashore would make for a smoother ride. I do believe we were both sipping bubbly, Carina from stemware, I from the bottle, when we finally made it ashore, to much laughter and cheering from our *Lost Colony* family. The weather was perfect that day, and even over twenty years later I can still smell the salt air and taste the mountains of crab and boiled corn, laid out on a newspaper-covered table and washed down with an ice-cold Heineken. That was the taste of absolute contentment.

— FRANK THOMPSON (1994)

Lightning Protocol, Everyone!

When inclement weather threatens, the crew must scramble to secure the ship. Photo by Delena Gray Ostrander

LAST NIGHT'S STORMS brought lightning strikes, and the technicians have been scrambling all day to cope with the damage. The backstage monitors are not functioning, meaning no one can hear what is happening onstage, so David Bost and Jake Newcomb are stringing fresh cables. David has sprained his hand and wrapped it in an Ace bandage, and he awkwardly carries an extension ladder from speaker to speaker in hopes of restoring sound. As he sweats in his black show clothes, I see his black tortoise-shell glasses have slipped down to the tip of his nose. Stage management tells me the "God mic," used to address the audience, is out, too.

But the lion's share of the damage is to the costume shop. A bolt from the sky took out the power to the two air-conditioning units that chill the downstairs of the building, possibly damaging or destroying them. The second-floor unit has been cranked up, and strategically placed fans blow the cool air down the stairs from the production offices to the first floor, where the actors are dressed and fitted and where the wardrobe stitchers hand-paint the designs on the Native Americans. Worse still, every computer in the building is, to one extent or another, fried; costumers and stage managers must use their cell phones to access notes.

But worst of all, one of the strikes to the costume shop traveled "downstream" to the light shack and killed two control units for LEDs and moving lights. The LEDs blend three primary colors in various intensities to create the desired shadings of the rainbow, but now everything is only white. These sealed control units can only be replaced, not repaired, so tonight's big show will be very pale and bright.

The outdoor venue lends its own drama to *The Lost Colony*. Photo courtesy of *The Lost Colony*

"Never a dull moment around these parts," says Bri Weintraub as she chugs a bottle of water before going back to work. She has her gear on as well as her backstage radio. It crackles and she charges off purposefully to another part of the theater. Two other electricians are climbing the proscenium wall on stage right, their arms looping and grabbing on to the lighting positions like they are two kids on the monkey bars of a jungle gym.

"It's the male end that you need," says Sydney Norris to Monika Cruson. They are testing the control cables.

"Kelsy, tie the boat down and put the sails away," says Johnny Underwood to Kelsy Sedmak as he looks nervously at the radar app on his phone. "We're about to get smacked."

The stage managers confabulating backstage break huddle and scatter in different directions.

"Lightning protocol, everyone!" yells stage-right assistant stage manager Dennis McGinnis, at which the electricians descend from their perches and everyone disappears indoors.

The company instituted a lightning protocol several years after I last did this show. It simply means that if a lightning strike is detected within five miles, everyone in the theater, whether audience or company, needs to be indoors for the next fifteen minutes.

Photo courtesy of *The Lost Colony*

"I hope it doesn't rain," says a choir member as he looks out of the dressing room. "My parents are here tonight."

Pillows of clouds are piling up southwest of the theater, and the high, flat outflows from the thunderheads sail directly overhead, reaching off toward the northeast like fingers. Across the water to the north, individual squalls pour silent rain into the sound. They look harmless enough, but only a week ago the clouds joined to form waterspouts that marched ashore at Colington Island. Years ago, I saw three waterspouts dancing like cobras as they marched up the sound from Manns Harbor toward Currituck. They moved in a line, writhing obscenely back and forth and undulating hideously from side to side.

Johnny Underwood and Dennis McGinnis climb to the top of the stage-right parapet and look into the approaching storm. Johnny points at something, and then suddenly, as they appraise their situation, a rainbow arcs against the dark clouds above their heads. The sun is setting; it is below the cloud line, flooding the backstage with furious white light.

The actors take turns at the doorway so they can snap pictures of Johnny and Dennis and the rainbow on their cell phones. The show is canceled at 8:35 P.M. due to lightning.

If a lightning strike is detected within five miles, everyone in the theater, whether audience or company, needs to be indoors for the next fifteen minutes.

One of my favorite *Lost Colony* memories was from July 20, 1969. It was my first year working at *The Lost Colony*. I had just graduated from high school and was thrilled to be a professional (!) in this play I'd grown up seeing probably since I was seven or eight. Anything that needed to be done, I'd do it! Joe Layton and Bob Knowles appreciated my enthusiasm and gave me a lot to do in the show, little things, yes, but things that added color and richness to a scene. Layton was known for that. Later that summer, we were presenting a Masque in the Elizabethan Gardens on Sunday, July 20. William Ivey Long was in charge of designing all the costumes for the Masque, and as my roommates were all costumers, they had been working diligently with him for this very special presentation. After the show was over Saturday night, acknowledging there was still a lot to do to be ready for the Masque, Billy Long instructed them to come over to his parents' house in Manteo to finish up on the costumes for the next day. Billy was an old family friend, and I knew how to sew, so I joined my roommates over there to help finish what needed to be done for the next day's performance. We were all pretty tired after a full week of doing the show, but we kept working conscientiously until about 3 A.M., when Billy said, "Stop. We need to go outside." We didn't know what he was doing, but we put our fabrics down and followed him out to the backyard. "Look up," he said. And then he said that this night our astronauts were on the moon, and we needed to honor the moment. We all stood there in the quiet of the night with a gentle breeze passing, humbly looking up at the moon, feeling very small and yet overwhelmed at what was happening. I will never forget it.

— TALMADGE RAGAN (1969–1972)

Note: On July 20, 1969, as part of the Apollo 11 mission, Neil Armstrong and Buzz Aldrin became the first humans to land on the moon.

The View from the Light Shack

A WEEK LATER, I watch the show from the light shack for the first time.

"How we doin' stage left?" asks production stage manager Jennifer Gregory into her headset, swiveling her rolling office chair to face the multipaned window on the second floor of the light shack. Stage-right assistant stage manager Dennis McGinnis has already confirmed the actors on the men's dressing room side are in their places.

"We're ready," replies ASM Sarah Dove, her disembodied voice sounding from a small speaker mounted on the wall.

"Stand by, everyone," Jennifer says, switching off the speaker so the reports from backstage come through only her black headset. Sitting in a small rolling chair behind her, I see she has her curly, dark hair tied loosely in a bun on the back of her head, and while it is warm in the booth it is not unpleasant. But as she opens the large window in front of her small wooden desk, locking it in position, a blast of hot, muggy air slaps my face like a wet washcloth. Jennifer feels it, too, and tells me that the temperature at show time is 99 degrees; half an hour ago, it was 102. Heat protocol number two is in effect, meaning the actors will wear no hats or bonnets or capes during this evening's show. Inside the booth, a small white oscillating fan sits on the floor at Jennifer's feet, sweeping back and forth, hitting me with what might be loosely termed a breeze when it bends my way. A seven-foot-tall stack of gently whirring electronics known as "repeaters" stands beside her desk between her and Monika Cruson, the light board operator.

The recorded announcements signal that the show is about to begin; impressively, the audience applauds. It will be a good show when a house

An old theatrical joke says that while a director might think he is God, the stage manager actually is God.

The production stage manager (in 2017, Jennifer Gregory) oversees the show from the light shack behind the audience seating area. Even during the mayhem of the battle scenes, the stage manager calls cues in a voice that barely rises above a whisper. Photo by Ira David Wood III

responds like that in this heat. Actors live for that sound. Inside the booth, however, it is as quiet as a library. The production stage manager whispers cues into a microphone an inch from her face. The sound montage swells, then fades as the Historian emerges from the trees.

"Stand by for fog . . . Go . . . Lights 11.5. Go."

From the next room, I hear the metallic hiss of an iris opening on a follow spot. The show has three of these massive instruments, each one operated manually by an electrician on a headset. The iris is a feature of the instrument

that allows the operator to either narrow the light beam tightly on the face or to open it loosely on the full body of the actor. To extinguish the light completely is to "douse" it with another control switch blocking the beam totally. Years ago, when I ran follow spots for WWE, we had filters to add color—red for the wrestler Kane, for example—but there are no colored spots in this show, only white lights to illuminate the principal actors onstage.

After the Prologue choir recedes into the trees stage right, the follow spot tracks the Historian, Don Bridge, onto the mainstage as the Indian Dance

The stage manager serves as the director's eyes and ears from the light shack and makes sure the show runs smoothly. Photo by Delena Gray Ostrander

begins. In this break from her cues, Jennifer has a few seconds to speak to me.

"I hear you have three hundred cues in the show," I say softly, even though it would be impossible to hear us outside the building.

"I don't know. I'll have to count them sometime," she replies, swiveling in her chair to face me and covering her headset mic with her hand. "Sure, we have cues like 11 or 12 or 13, but we also have cues within cues, like 11.5, or 12.1 or .2 or .3, and they have to happen quickly, so I don't have time to give warnings."

As I am about to ask another question, she holds up her hand and swivels back to face the show. On the desk in front of her are a pad and pen, and she scribbles furiously for a few seconds, calling cues at the same time.

The pad and pen are for show notes. If an actor misses blocking or drops lines, he or she will hear about it after the show, and there are often technical issues to be corrected. With director Ira David Wood gone, the production stage manager runs this show on a day-to-day basis, giving life to an old theatrical joke saying that while a director might think he is God, the stage manager actually *is* God.

Looking around the booth, I see rows of shelves on one of the raw plywood walls with thick notebooks stacked on top of each other, bibles for the show's operations. Cardboard boxes sit stacked in the corners. Replacement parabolic reflector lamps, essentially old automobile headlights, sit in plastic bins. Coils of cables and loose cords lie on the floor and on hooks on the walls. Behind me on a table, a single white coffee mug holds down a pile of papers on the cutting board used for chopping the colored gels that every hanging instrument used to need. Small precision patterns cut into thin sheets of steel called "gobos" hang on the wall, too. If you insert a gobo into a lighting instrument, you can project patterns, such as tree limbs or prison bars, or shapes, such as animals or a crescent moon. Despite being steel, gobos are notoriously delicate; even single oily fingerprints will destroy them once subjected to the intense heat inside lighting instruments. Gloves must be worn when handling them.

Halfway through Act I, Jennifer casually flips on the overhead lights in the booth so she can see to write notes. The sky is pink now, and the water of the sound over the parapet is the color of sharkskin.

Jennifer has four channels to call cues on: on channel one, she speaks directly to Jake Newcomb on sound, who mans the board at the top of the house; on channel two, she speaks to lights, the three follow-spot ops, and Monika Cruson on the light board; channel four is costumes, in case a quick-change goes horribly wrong; channel three is for the backstage stage managers. She keeps Dennis McGinnis and Sarah Dove on the open channel of a hand-held cordless radio in case of a backstage emergency. During the show, she switches from channel to channel as needed.

High up on a corner of one shelf, I see a two-toned antique microphone about a foot and a half tall that looks like something Walter Cronkite might have sat in front of; freestanding and aerodynamic, it has a heavy look, as if it could double as a weapon.

"Is that the God mic?" The God mic is what she uses to make announcements to the audience.

*M*y brother, Buddy, and I were "wards" of Ruth Thompson, so we went to rehearsals of the show during the days and sometimes had to go during performances. We loved to sit right in front and watch Foster Fitz-Simmons do his high jump. Then we'd scoot over to the choir loft and watch when Don Somers (Old Tom) would spit his "Plymouth Ale" in a big spray on the choir, who couldn't move. Johnny Long was my best friend, and when the governor was saying his farewell, and then John Borden (I particularly remember Gordon Clark), on accepting his promotion, spoke of "a new nation," I was so clever with my ad lib, "our nation," and Johnny would murmur, "damnation." It was all I could do to not crack up. Loved that Johnny.

—MARY JOLLIFF MOORE (1961–63, late 1960s–70s, 1987, 1990s)

"No, that's the backstage mic. The God mic is there," she says, pointing to a small black zippered case beside it. "It's cordless."

What is so surprising is just how quiet and collected it is up here. I had expected chaos, which is what I remember from being backstage, but the booth is full of calm, hushed tones. The difference is night and day. Even during the mayhem that defines the Big Battle, when Jennifer has the most cues to call, her voice barely rises above a whisper.

A couple of days later, while visiting again with retired choreographer Johnny Walker, I mention how calm it was.

"The booth?" He laughs. "That's where Roz MacEnulty and I played cards while we listened to the show. We listened to the rhythm. If the rhythm of the show was right, that meant the show was right." He pauses to laugh again and then says, "When Lynn Lockrow was stage manager, he watched the show through binoculars to make sure no one was goofing around."

If an actor misses blocking or drops lines, he or she will hear about it after the show, and there are often technical issues to be corrected.

Waiting in the wings. Photo by Delena Gray Ostrander

The Bard on Roanoke Island

SHAKESPEARE'S IMPRINT on the American psyche is as indelible as the King James Bible. Alexis de Tocqueville, when touring America in the 1830s, remarked, "There is hardly a pioneer's hut that does not contain a few odd volumes of Shakespeare. I remember reading the feudal drama of *Henry V* for the first time in a log cabin." Tonight, late Saturday night, after post-show showers and maybe a quick nosh, everyone makes their way down to the sound stage to see the Professional Theater Workshop's production of Shakespeare's *Twelfth Night*.

For the past two weeks, ten actors and almost as many technicians have juggled work calls and day jobs and PR appearances during the day and fought post-show exhaustion at night to rehearse this show, sometimes going as late as two in the morning. They have sweated and labored and sacrificed, and tonight is the night, the single night to shine, for other than the children's show, PTW performances are one-time events. Towering thunderstorms canceled tonight's big show, but another kind of electricity is in the air now, and the buzz of anticipation surrounding this show is good. I hear that something extraordinary is about to happen.

Inside the sound stage, rows of folding chairs surround three sides of the low platforms, forming a thrust stage. There are no elaborate set pieces, just the sky drop from the children's show framed by drapery. Company members take their seats and sip drinks from plastic cups or water bottles and look through the printed program while I find a seat next to Pam Atha.

"Do you like Shakespeare?" she asks.

"I love Shakespeare," I say.

"I don't," she says matter-of-factly. "So if I nod off, be sure and elbow me in the ribs."

The comedy *Twelfth Night* is a charming piece of fluff based on mistaken identities: Brother and sister twins are separated in a shipwreck. While the sister assumes the disguise of a man, her brother wanders the land, thinking her dead. She falls in love with the duke she serves, the countess whom the duke courts falls in love with her, and three drunken servants forge a letter to further muddy the waters. In the end, when the masks are lifted and all is revealed, brother and sister are reunited, true lovers are joined, and rude pranksters get their just desserts. A more contrived story could not be invented by a Hollywood hack, and that outlandishness is exactly what makes this modest production so superlative. This is not low budget; this is no budget, and I am blown away.

Sir Toby Belch is a cheap, drunken disco king in polyester. Sir Andrew Aguecheek is a cowardly Urkel in pink socks and a bow tie. When the radiant countess Olivia strides across the stage with her long blond hair pouring over her fur coat, she looks ready for the catwalk, and the twins have identical costumes to help the audience make the connection. The sourpuss Malvolio is lured into wearing a disastrous black teddy with yellow stockings. There are musical interludes and brief dances, sword fights and slapstick. Handy black umbrellas serve to suggest scenery that neither time nor money can provide.

But most remarkable are the performances by these young actors. I never lose them in the script, and they never stumble over words; indeed, they excel at their craft, pulling me into the emotional mess that is Shakespeare in love. When I worked for the North Carolina Shakespeare Festival in High Point, I saw what heights could be attained when his scripts were staged by full-time professional performers and technicians. Watching the show unfold in front of my eyes like some theatrical moonflower, I cannot help wondering what this production could be with financial backing; instead of a single, bare-bones, late-night kamikaze run of screaming laughter, it could be much, much more. If nothing else, the risers would not creak.

For the past two weeks, ten actors and almost as many technicians have juggled work calls and day jobs and PR appearances during the day and fought post-show exhaustion at night to rehearse this show, sometimes going as late as two in the morning.

The cast and crew members who participate in Professional Theater Workshop productions juggle work calls, evening performances, and outside jobs. The cast of *Twelfth Night* rehearsed for two weeks to stage a single performance of the Shakespeare play. Photo by Jamil Zraikat

I never have to elbow Pam Atha in the ribs.

A couple of days later, rounding the corner of the dressing room, I find Ethan and Caitlyn straddling a bench, sitting face to face, reading Shakespeare to each other from their phones. Ethan Lyvers plays John Borden in the big show, and choir member Caitlyn Leach is the tap-dancing gourmet pirate from the children's show. Both were in the PTW production of *Twelfth Night*.

"Are you rehearsing?" I ask when they seem to reach a stopping point.

"No, we're just having fun," Ethan says, as if noticing me for the first time.

"We're just a couple of Shakespeare dorks," Caitlyn laughs.

"How did you arrive at the decision to produce *Twelfth Night*?" I ask Ethan. He co-directed the production with Emily Asbury, who plays Queen Elizabeth in the big show.

"Emily said, 'You should do a Shakespeare so I can do it with you,' so I submitted the proposal, and they said yes."

Broadway Comes to Waterside Theatre

The Lost Colony, born in the summer of 1937, was a changed show when it arose phoenix-like from the big fire of 1947, and the energy and drive wrung from the living memory of that fire sustained the show through the end of the 1950s, when attendance began to falter ominously.

In 1962, RIHA elected Washington, D.C., social maven Emma Neal Morrison as its chairperson. It was Morrison who secured the funds to buy the land to erect the company housing that bears her name today, and it was Emma Neal Morrison who persuaded Broadway fixture Joe Layton to remake the production in 1964. Layton's show was a triumph.

For twenty years, from 1964 to 1984, Joe Layton was the director and choreographer of *The Lost Colony*, and his artistic imprint is still on this show. It was Layton who integrated the choir members into the action onstage and demolished their loft; it was Layton who took the microphone from the Historian and turned him out of his booth. Layton's sense of showmanship filled the vast space, and his fluid staging heightened emotional levels. He collaborated closely with Paul Green to cut much of the liturgy from the script, accelerating the action. His show was one of constant motion, and his integration of disparate theatrical elements, including completely redesigned scenery, realized a new concept of what the show could be, taking it to a higher plane. Layton's dynamic vision was hailed by all, including Paul Green, when it debuted in 1964. Current

Joe Layton, pictured with Melissa Manchester and Barbra Streisand, brought new energy and excitement to *The Lost Colony* when he was named director in 1964. Photo courtesy of *The Lost Colony*

It was Emma Neal Morrison who persuaded Broadway fixture Joe Layton to remake the production in 1964.

director Ira David Wood cites Layton's production as inspiration for his own direction of the show.

Six foot five and all legs, Layton was a New Yorker who started singing as a kid at the Catskills resorts his family frequented. He debuted on Broadway at age sixteen as a dancer in *Oklahoma*. But even as he won awards for his direction and choreography, he referred to himself as a "stager." He staged four TV concerts for Barbra Streisand; he staged portions of the 1984 Olympics; he moved gracefully and effortlessly from Cher to Siegfried and Roy to Richard Pryor to Willie Nelson and many, many more. And although this line of work dictated a peripatetic lifestyle, Layton called Roanoke Island home, and his son, Jeb, went to school here. Robert Midgette mentored Jeb at Manteo Middle School.

I find general agreement among those who knew him well that upon the death of his wife, Evelyn, Joe Layton lost his rudder. He and the show drifted away from each other, finally parting ways after the 1984 season. For many who remember his work, *The Lost Colony* had some of its finest years during Joe Layton's run.

Dr. Fred W. Morrison and Emma Neal Morrison were generous benefactors of *The Lost Colony* for many years. Mrs. Morrison served 20 years as producer of the show and chaired the Roanoke Island Historical Assocation for 12 years. Photo courtesy of *The Lost Colony*

The Tamer of Darkness, Fire, and Flood

IN AUGUST 1960, Hurricane Donna was a classic long-track storm with winds of over one hundred miles per hour. After forming off Cape Verde, it knocked about the Caribbean and smacked Florida before roaring north, making landfall near Cape Fear during the second week of September, pushing a wall of water up the Pamlico Sound before passing over Roanoke Island. One reporter at the time described Donna as "the storm with the beautiful eye," an eye between fifty and eighty miles wide with a clearly visible moon among scudding clouds. For *The Lost Colony*, it was a disaster.

Alone at the top of the house, Skipper Bell chewed his cigar and quietly waited for the wall of water he knew was coming.

There is a story, possibly apocryphal, that Skipper Bell made his way to the theater to ride out the storm. Alone at the top of the house, he chewed his cigar and quietly waited for the wall of water he knew was coming. In a few short hours, the waters of the sound rose somewhere between four and eight feet above normal, engulfing Waterside Theatre. The National Weather Service recorded a six-foot storm surge at Oregon Inlet.

Pushed and pulled by the wind and the water, the buoyant lumber of the theater worked itself free from where it was nailed. The loose lumber beat against the structures, weakening them further, until the backstage and then the mainstage began to come apart. Donna wrecked over ten thousand square feet of Waterside Theatre, from the dressing rooms to the cabins. The undermined Chapel almost collapsed backward into the sound. For years afterward, people stepped on lighting instruments if they went swimming backstage. But once again, Irene Rains saved the costumes; she had the foresight to have them removed to higher ground before the storm hit.

Flood waters from Hurricane Donna in 1960 destroyed much of Waterside Theatre. Photo: David Stick Collection, Outer Banks History Center

Albert Quentin "Skipper" Bell, architect and savior of Waterside Theatre. Photo: David Stick Collection, Outer Banks History Center

With patchwork construction, Skipper Bell cobbled the theater back together in time for the 1961 season. Thanks to funds contributed directly or raised indirectly by Emma Neal Morrison, RIHA had enough money in 1962 to completely remodel Waterside Theatre. Skipper Bell, the man who moved to the Outer Banks because he "thought the place was bloody tropical," died in September 1964. The "tamer of darkness, fire, and flood" is buried on Roanoke Island.

A Staggering Loss

IN THE EARLY HOURS of Tuesday, September 11, 2007, a resident of Villa Dunes in Nags Head looked across the dark waters of the sound and decided something was not right. She had seen the brightly lit theater during the summer and unconsciously noted its regularity, but *The Lost Colony* had closed for the season more than two weeks ago. Yet where there should have been only darkness marking the north end of Roanoke Island on this clear, starry night, there was bright orange light. She promptly picked up the phone and called 911 to report "what looks like a huge fire" at *The Lost Colony*. It was 12:35 A.M. Every fire department north of Oregon Inlet responded.

On September 11, 2007, fire destroyed the costume shop and everything in it—including nearly all the costumes dating back to the original production. Photo courtesy of *The Lost Colony*

Carl Curnutte, the executive director at the time, recalls getting a phone call from the 911 operator, who had been a house manager for *The Lost Colony*. "She said, 'I thought you would want to know there's been a report of a fire,'" says Curnutte. She couldn't tell him exactly where the fire was, just that it was somewhere in Fort Raleigh National Historic Site.

The Roanoke Island Volunteer Fire Department, led by Captain Kenny Peckrun, arrived backstage at *The Lost Colony* to find the forty-one-hundred-square-foot, two-story Irene Smart Rains Costume Pavilion completely ablaze. Flames poured from the first- and second-story windows, topping even the trees. The men's dressing room, only a matter of yards from the open flames,

Not only were more than a thousand active show costumes lost, but another five hundred to a thousand retired, conserved, or replacement costumes disappeared in the flames, some original to the 1937 production.

was ready to ignite. Firefighters immediately set up a water curtain to cool the exposed end and roof of the single-story structure.

"That was our main concern," Peckrun said later. "If it got that, I feel pretty strongly that we would've lost the theater."

"It burned so fast [the firefighters] were afraid it was going to move on into the dressing rooms," says Curnutte. "They knew the costume shop was lost, so they focused on trying to save the dressing rooms, and they did an amazing job."

Unable to enter the burning building safely, firefighters battled the inferno from without for an hour and a half before declaring it under control, confining it to the costume shop and two small maintenance and storage sheds, thus preventing a general conflagration backstage. The costume shop burned down to the sand. It was only ten years old. The cause of the fire has never been determined.

The losses were staggering: Not only were more than a thousand active show costumes lost, but another five hundred to a thousand retired, conserved, or replacement costumes disappeared in the flames, some of them one of a kind from previous seasons, some original to the 1937 production. Whole rolls of cloth and bolts of fabric, boxes of buttons and snaps, hooks and eyes, needles and scissors, bonnets and hats, capes and shoes, wigs and crowns, all went up in smoke. Steel swords and armor melted to slag.

Carl Curnutte, then executive director of *The Lost Colony,* inspects the damage from the 2007 fire. Photo courtesy of *The Lost Colony*

BACKSTAGE AT *THE LOST COLONY*

William Ivey Long and his staff recreated more than 1,000 costumes in less than ten months—just in time for the 2008 season. Photo by Duane Cochran

The boat, which was parked by the costume shop, was incinerated. Inside the blackened footprint of the building, the charred carcasses of half a dozen sewing machines sat upright in filthy sand where they had fallen through the burning floorboards. Drawings and models, renderings and designs, records and photos going back seventy years disappeared forever.

"It was a great loss," says Curnutte, whose time with the show began in 1989 as a wardrobe stitcher. "What I saw more than anything were the people who wore all those costumes. Having been a costumer, fitting the actors, and getting to know them all summer long and experiencing the summer with them, I saw countless individuals that we all knew over the different years with *The Lost Colony*."

Relief came almost immediately in the form of donations; by the end of October, the National Park Service and the State of North Carolina pledged half a million dollars each to the restoration of the physical plant. Grassroots fundraising drives such as "Dimes for Drama" and "Cookies for Colonists" popped up overnight. Over two hundred individuals and organizations contacted *The Lost Colony* offering to help.

"So many people helped, right down to the little girl who gave her tooth fairy money."

Terry Clark, a former *Colony* properties master, was warehouse manager on HBO's miniseries *John Adams* at the time; she arranged for her show to donate costumes after it wrapped, as did Janet Melody, who was working in Wilmington on a film about jazz musician Buddy Bolden. To alter these and other lovingly donated items, a temporary costume shop was set up in the apartments of Morrison Grove. Andy Griffith donated the sword he had worn as Sir Walter half a century earlier, a sword presented to him by RIHA.

"So many people helped, right down to the little girl who gave her tooth fairy money," says Curnutte. "It was refreshing to see people come together and rally behind the production."

By a quirk of fate, some of the most intricate and expensive costumes were hundreds of miles away on the mainland. One of Queen Elizabeth's dresses was in Wilmington at the Cameron Art Museum, and Sir Walter Raleigh's

Andy Griffith joined the cast and crew to celebrate the completion of the rebuilt costume shop. To his right is John Wilson, the Manteo architect who designed the building. Photo by J. Aaron Trotman

costume was on display at the North Carolina Museum of History. A handful of delicately stitched courtier costumes were at a dry cleaner. But that was it; all the Native American garb, every colonist costume, every Red Soldier uniform would have to be made from scratch.

Despite the extreme pressure to re-create costumes in time for the coming season, William Ivey Long saw an opportunity. "I started by working with lebame houston, the historian for RIHA, and we gathered the roster of people on the ship that sailed to Roanoke, and spent many months researching who these people were, and why they chose to leave England for an unknown world," he said. "The biggest discovery was the disproportionate number of upper-class people on the voyage. This ultimately meant fewer people to plow fields, plant crops, build houses, and do the other manual labor needed. This also likely contributed to the demise of the settlement. It was a huge moment for me that, after several decades of living with this story, I saw the entire enterprise in a new light. I then designed costumes for different classes of people, which not only is more visually varied but also more strongly tells the story of this first English settlement in the New World."

By Thanksgiving, the renderings for the new costumes went to the many different shops and individual builders assigned to reconstitute the wardrobe. Shops outside the state received whole cloth and returned finished pieces. Locals such as Pixie Westcott and Joan Brumbach worked overtime on the island. Curnutte, whose energy and drive spearheaded the rebuilding effort, helped cut the ribbon for a new costume shop in April, rebuilt with relatively few changes to the design Manteo architect John Wilson created for the building that had burned. "I don't think people really realized the toll it took on the staff at that time. It was a rough six months," says Curnutte.

The sewing would continue all summer, but the show that opened that May shone more brightly than it had in years.

"It was a huge moment for me that, after several decades of living with this story, I saw the entire enterprise in a new light."

Virginia Dare Night

Tonight is for the five little Virginia Dares who wait unknowingly in the air conditioning, and for one little Virginia who was born 430 years ago.

AT SETUP ON THIS, the eighteenth day of August, steamy air yields a gentle shower while the sun plays peekaboo behind the clouds. After a sweltering fight call, tanned ATs wear only what they must: shorts and work shoes, stripped down to the waist or strapped into sports bras, all of them soaked with sweat from the heat and humidity. The softly falling rain is no nuisance; the precipitation is cooling, and these people have a job to do. The sweat and the rain mingle, rolling off everyone in streams while they set up the show on Swirly Girl's birthday.

"I had an alcoholic frog last night," says a shirtless, bearded AT carrying the back half of a parapet flat.

"Oh yeah?" asks his shirtless, bearded partner on the front half. They steady the plywood and canvas beast, pausing in front of the props cabin to sling the flat over their heads casually in preparation for the charge up the parapet stairs. "Alcoholic Frog? Is that a drink?"

"No, there was a frog in my drink," says the back half of the duo.

"What was he doing there?"

"Just chillin'," he says as they both charge up the steps at full speed.

Tonight, *The Lost Colony* honors its own; the most promising, the most professional, the best of the best receive awards in the names of men and women who have given decades of service to this show, awards bearing the names of Basnight and Fearing and Midgette and Knowles and Layton. Producer Bill Coleman assembles the company onstage in front of the audience and calls them up one by one to be acknowledged. The applause from the house is more than polite. The assembled company loudly cheers each one; after a summer of working together, they know these outstanding people genuinely deserve recognition on this special night.

It is fitting and proper to acknowledge them tonight, for August 18, 1587, was Virginia Dare's birth date, and tonight is Live Baby Night at *The Lost Colony*. Even now, the wee ones are backstage, corralled in a playpen inside the air-conditioned costume shop. Long ago, the company learned that lots of parents wanted their babies to debut on this stage. And make no mistake, proud parents come from many miles away to have Eleanor sing their child a lullaby, or to have Father Martin christen them Virginia. One couple drove with their child from Cary, North Carolina. There is even a sort of informal audition process. Fussy babies and crying babies need not apply. Night owls are preferred.

Ten-month-old Kinslee Grace Davis, shown with Henson Milam as Eleanor Dare and Daniel Dutot as Ananias Dare, was one of five babies to go on stage as Virginia Dare during the 80th production season. Photo courtesy of *The Lost Colony*

Little Virginia Dare is in five scenes in the second act, so five babies will go on tonight, including Malcolm Fearing's grandchild. But probably the proudest of the proud is Don Bridge, who plays the Historian in this year's show, because his grandchild is the Final March baby and will go up the ramp in Eleanor's arms.

"I'm not going to take her in the tunnel," Pam Atha tells stage management, referring to a piece of the standard choreography in the Christening Dance. "There's too much traffic."

Strict protocols are in place for Live Baby Night; if you have no direct stage business with the children, stage management shoos you away, instructing you firmly to go sit on a bench. There is also a heat protocol for tonight's show; the actors perform without hats or bonnets or capes, but the wee ones are kept comfortably cool in the costume shop, where parents swap stories and change diapers, waiting for a stage manager to call their cue. And the babies get bigger, too, as the show progresses; the Final Assembly baby has her little feet sticking out from underneath Eleanor's arms, as does Don's grandchild in the Final March.

Before the show, there are last-minute problems. Backstage right, the batteries for the mics are not properly charged. Just when it appears there will be no mic check, thunder sounds from the sky and stage management instructs

I was in the group of colonists that sides with the Runner right before Final March. I was standing by Eleanor's Cabin right before the freeze that takes place as the Historian speaks. Right before that happens, my job is to pull the crib out so that Denise Dalton [in the role of a colonist woman] can grab the baby Virginia doll out to give it to Madeline Rains as Eleanor Dare. After the doll was out, I picked up the crib and put it on my shoulder and marched up the hill. Well, the doll was very old, and the head was coming loose. We had told the props master, who decided that she would duct-tape the head back on. So that night, as Madeline, Denise, and I were standing around the crib, the doll head comes off the body and lands in the crib with a very loud thump. We all had to stifle our laughter so as not to give away what happened, as the audience could not see it with us blocking it. After the freeze, Denise tried to grab the head back out of the crib. Madeline said, "Just give me the body," and arranged the blanket so you couldn't see the headless doll. As I carried the crib up the hill, the doll head thumped in my ear as it rolled back and forth in the crib on every step. Madeline had to pose in the spotlight holding the baby as she stood with John Borden, and she was maintaining well, but I could see the straining in her eyes as I passed by. When I came offstage, I asked the stage-right manager, Frank Mack, if he wanted a baby head and handed him the doll head out of the crib. I remember him saying, "Well, that's not right."

— STEVEN GRAINGER (1988, 1990–91)

everyone to observe the lightning protocol and go indoors, which buys time for the batteries to charge while the work has stopped. At 6:51 P.M., when the all clear sounds and preshow setup resumes, the batteries have enough charge to test before they go back to the charging station.

Backstage left, props assistant Emma Anderson repairs the broken bottom on one of Old Tom's water buckets. With only half an hour before show time, the fix will be down and dirty. She deftly attaches a block to the inside, which she then screws to the broken bottom, and in five minutes the prop is ready for the show. This late in the season, the bucket will not be replaced. Nor will the mate to it, which is just as rotten and ready to split any second. It is a temporary fix.

Temporary things have a way of becoming permanent at *The Lost Colony*. In 1998, I found a load-bearing post being held in place by a single two-inch-long finish nail. It had been fastened that way for a long time—several years, judging by the rust—and I still wonder how it came to be. It could have been an oversight; someone tacked it in place and then forgot to come back and nail it off. Maybe it was a low-priority problem at the end of some night years earlier.

But not tonight, for tonight is Live Baby Night, and tonight is for the five little Virginia Dares who wait unknowingly in the air conditioning, and for one little Virginia born 430 years ago. The company responds beautifully; they feel it, too. The show simply glows.

At intermission, I see Marjalene Thomas and ask how she handled unruly babies onstage when she played Eleanor.

"I had my charms," she says with a smile. She then reaches to the top of her blouse and pulls out a set of thin gold necklaces. Small *Lost Colony* pendants and medallions flash in the light, making soft tinkling sounds. "If I had a distracted baby, I just held her with one hand and jingled these in front of her with the other. Did the trick every time."

John Underwood (center), technical director, receives the 2017 Bradford Fearing Producers Award from RIHA CEO and producer Bill Coleman (left) and associate producer Lance Culpepper. Photo courtesy of *The Lost Colony*

Every summer on August 18, *The Lost Colony* marks the birth of Virginia Dare, the first English child born in the New World. In 2017, the role of Father Martin was played by Nicholas Baggarley. Photo by Eden Saunders, Busy B Photography

By eerie coincidence, an event took place here that few mark on their calendars. On this very date in 1590, three years to the day after his granddaughter Virginia was born, John White arrived on Roanoke Island with his long-delayed relief expedition, only to find the fort deserted, his family gone forever into the oblivion of the Croatan wilderness. I can only imagine what must have gone through his mind when the boom of his signal cannon echoed across the water unanswered.

AT THE FINISH OF PRESHOW fight call on closing night, fight director Robert Midgette stops the actors in place. A light rain is falling again.

"We're going to do it one more time . . . ," he says.

"*Uno mas.* One more time," say the obedient combatants without enthusiasm. They clap their hands anyway.

". . . but this time, put your props away and just have fun with it!"

Robert has their attention now, and they scurry to put props away and set for the only slapstick fight they have had all summer. No one cares about the rain.

Jake Newcomb in the sound booth cues the music, and the farcical battle is joined: immediately after the first arrow flies, the upstage choir begins disco dancing; an actor with a Mohawk taps a colonist on the shoulder and with a polite "Excuse me" stabs him over and over again; an actor is shot center stage and falls into the sand flopping like a fish in the bottom of a boat or a piece of bacon sizzling in a pan; Ananias Dare uses his cell phone as his sword; one Indian goes to kill a colonist but instead takes her in his arms and kisses her deeply like that famous photo of the couple in Times Square on V-J Day; one man is about to kill another when he drops to one knee and offers a pantomime ring in a wedding proposal. Willy-nilly running is required, silly walks rule, and shirts and hats and shoes fly through the air. I laugh until I cry.

Backstage for the preshow setup, the rain has picked up. A flat glides by me onstage.

"It's raining again," says a bearded face toward the front of the flat.

"Good," replies a bearded face toward the back. "Maybe it will hide my tears."

Backstage by the costume shop, company members take last-minute pictures with friends while the choir warms up. As they sing softly through one

As the season draws to a close, the final scenes feel more emotional to many members of the company—and often to the audience as well. Photo by Eden Saunders, Busy B Photography

song, one of the little colonist girls comes running up to Caitlyn Leach and presents her with a big bag of candy.

"I got these for you!" she chirps to the whole group. "You can have them on the drive home!" She pulls supersized packages of Kit Kats and of gummy bears out of her bag as if it were Halloween turned upside down, where kids give candy to adults.

"You got these for us?" asks Caitlyn, who played the tap-dancing gourmet pirate from the kiddie show. She raises her hands to her mouth and starts to cry. "We'll sing for you."

A few quick words fly among the adults; the leader marks the time, and then the choir launches into a flawless rendition of the opening number to *The Lion King*. The little colonist girl clenches her hands together over her chest, enraptured, her sweet young face a picture of adoration.

And then, just like that, the last show is over.

Afterward, the backstage is unnaturally quiet. People passing each other speak in hushed voices, as if all sound has been drained from the air, leaving a void. Every few minutes, a war whoop erupts from the Indian dressing room, announcing that another Mohawk has been shaved. While I wait for the cast to change out of their costumes for the last time, Sir Walter Raleigh walks by me in street clothes, his freshly shaven chin jutting out pale and white in the backstage light. I do a double take when I recognize him.

Walking past the brightly lit shop, I see David Bost, the assistant sound engineer, sitting alone. He stares straight ahead, contemplating, looking at nothing, ignoring me and the work spread out in front of him on a low table.

"And just like that, it's over," I say to him.

He looks up at me with big, dark eyes and blinks a couple of times. "Huh?"

"It's over," I say again.

He rises, exhaling loudly. "And just like that, it's over. Just like that!" Then he launches into his post-show strike duties, saying again as he passes me, "It's over."

The freshly scalped Indians come out of the dressing room, each one sporting a bald head. Even in the dim light, the white stripes of skin running down the center of their heads are clearly visible, like someone painted them with a brush. The Mohawks were uncomfortable, so they told me. Fortunately for me, I will never know; I have only the memory of my irritating beard. The ATs with beards will shave in the Grove tonight.

Scraping and thudding come from onstage as an AT begins trenching the stage so that water will drain properly in a storm. Johnny Underwood walks out to stop him. The AT is fast; he digs almost to center before Johnny finally flags him down.

"Dude," he says with a grin as he stops him. Then he rubs his chin and laughs and says, "We don't need to do that tonight."

As the stunned AT walks off to put his shovel away, two other ATs walk onstage, one with a shovel and the other carrying a rake. The first AT stops them. "We don't need to do that tonight," he says with quiet authority.

Back at Morrison Grove after the show, there is a new vibe: that relaxed looseness that comes with finality. The show is over, and the company is breaking up. Although a few individuals have already departed for the academic world, returning earlier this week to their schools, most of the actors, singers, and dancers will flee to the mainland starting tomorrow morning. The costumers will stay an entire week longer to pack the clothes away. This is the last night they will be together as a full company, and tonight's entertainment at the communal picnic table is trying to recognize the choir and AT men as they descend the asphalt paths without their beards.

They come down in ones and twos, cleanly shaven for the first time in three months, their freshly washed, shaggy hair still wet but combed, bounding in with toothy smiles or slipping in quietly, their chins and jaw lines white and bright in the single harsh streetlight on the tall post in the center of the

Every few minutes, a war whoop erupts from the Indian dressing room, announcing that another Mohawk has been shaved.

This is the last night they will be together as a full company, and tonight's entertainment at the communal picnic table is trying to recognize the choir and AT men as they descend the asphalt paths without their beards.

common area. Here they stand, basking in the incomprehension of their soon-to-be ex-coworkers, playing one last prank.

The reaction is always the same. "Oh, my God! Is that really you?" they say over and over with wide eyes and gaping mouths, like some Greek chorus.

"I can't believe it! Look at you! I didn't even recognize you!" they say, covering their mouths with their hands.

The girls squeal with delight and tenderly touch the men's faces, as if to confirm they are real. The men laugh at each other, slap each other around, and joke about how weird their faces feel. The Indians have their fleshy, white-striped heads rubbed again and again. No one seems to remember that their pictures have been here the whole time in the souvenir program; no one says, "You look just like your head shot." It's as if they are seeing each other for the first time.

One of the last to enter the picnic area is Jamil Zraikat, who played Simon Fernando this summer, and he gets the biggest cheer by far. Jamil's head shot in the program shows him in a full beard, big and bushy, as if he had a cat wrapped around his face. He was an AT with that beard last year, too, so tonight is the first time almost anyone has seen him clean shaven. When he walks up the path, a young woman screams and throws her arms around him, and the whole company turns as one to gawk at him before a tremendous roar erupts. He joins the crowd with the happiest smile of them all.

It is easy to remark on how handsome they all look now that the beards are gone, and they are certainly that; nearly every one of them has leading-man good looks. But what is so amazing is how young they look in the pale light, because the simple act of shaving has taken years off them, as if they were reverse Rip Van Winkles who fell asleep to awaken young and beardless. They are as fresh and as full of promise as a new day, and tomorrow when they wake up they can look back and know they accomplished something in their young lives: they did *The Lost Colony*.

They look ready to take on the real world.

*M*y story with *The Lost Colony* goes back to the 1950s, when my grandparents took my mom, Bonnie Robertson (Lent), to see *The Lost Colony* as a child. She has a passion for history and later in life would work in archaeology at Jamestown. When I was cast as a dancer in 2004 and 2005, we spent two wonderful summers together in the cottage she and my father, Robert Lent, had built years earlier in Kill Devil Hills, while my father came down when he wasn't working. She helped by sewing my long colonist petticoat that needed to be fixed from the wear and tear of dancing in the sand. At 10:45 P.M., she would pause and know that I would be heading up that hill singing the Final March song—her favorite—along with the rest of the cast. And when we wanted to add some authentic Algonquian words while improvising chatter as Indians onstage, my mom, the ever-so-intelligent historian, wrote out flashcards with true Algonquian vocabulary. And all the Indian dancers would utilize it during the scene. I also have fond memories of the Indian Dance, choreographed by the wonderful Johnny Walker. We would perform a V movement with our arms. We named the movement "And the dream still lives!" and Johnny would stand in the back of the house [behind the audience] and replicate the arms along with us. It was so special! I will always feel at home at *The Lost Colony*. Maybe a future member of my own family will be a part of it one day.

—JENNIFER LENT (2004–5)

Strike

Backstage, the wigwams are on the move.

THE SCRAPE OF THE FLAT shovels onstage signals the start of strike Sunday morning. The nine o'clock sun is hot, but high clouds and a northwest breeze help alleviate the misery of the ATs moving sand out of the wings. Brooms swish behind them as the dune creeps toward center stage. By ten o'clock, the breeze dies and the clouds evaporate, leaving only the blazing sun.

"I'm sweatin' out alcohol," says a white-chinned face.

"I'm sooo hung over," another answers.

Neither of them even looks up, much less at each other, as they bend to the task at hand, the rhythmic scrape and swish-grunt-thud of ATs shoveling sand the only sounds. Then a ratchet gun in the wings sounds off like a blow to the head, followed by a loud thump.

"Whoa," says a voice casually from the scene dock. "That's good."

Roll-up doors on the two light towers clatter open. Within a minute, I see electricians wearing hardhats and do-rags and rigging harnesses inside both towers, and with the perfunctory cry of "Heads up!" the lowest circuiting cables start dropping to the ground. Scaffolding on the Queen's Stage goes up in a flash, and a crew begins removing the heavy crown moldings on the Queen's Chamber unit. This entire unit will be disassembled and put into storage. Another team of workers on the proscenium walls climbs ladders, carefully removing the painted scrims from the sound towers, exposing the rabbit wire backing that lets the scrims hold shape. After the wire mesh is removed, the speakers start coming down, too. ATs sweat under their hardhats.

Backstage, the wigwams are on the move. Some years, they overwinter in the rain shelters, but this year they will live backstage by the men's dressing room, since events have been scheduled for the theater. Prop bundles, carried

Photo by Kelsey Wright

by colonists during the show, line the railing to the boat track, soaking up sun before they go into storage in the lofts above the props cabins. All the flats move stage right; by consolidating them to this one scene dock, the other dock is free to store scenic elements for the off-season. Sometime before lunch, the costumers spread depression capes on the boat track railings. They stretch from dressing room to dressing room, freshly washed, drying in the midday sun.

The higher cables and lighting instruments start coming down from the towers while the ATs are at lunch. At the base of the lighting tower by the Indian Stage, I see Jake Johnson, a dancer and leader of the prefab Mo' Grove party crew. He stands shirtless in shorts and work shoes at the base of the tower, looking up with a hardhat locked squarely on his head. When lighting instruments and cables descend by rope from on high, he unlashes them, sets them to one side, then watches the rope go back up.

"I thought you were a dancer, Jake, not an electrician," I say to him in between lights.

"Johnny said he needed guys. I don't have to leave yet, so I stayed. I stayed on to help."

By two o'clock, the ATs are back from lunch, slathering on sunscreen and sucking down the last of their sodas before turning their attention to the boat. The masts must come down and go into storage.

"Everyone just do what you did before, only in reverse, and listen to Brandon [Cheney]," says Johnny Underwood.

At 2:24, the boat has no masts.

Photo by Duane Cochran

A Symbol of Endurance

The "Dare Venus" has a history as rich and tempestuous as the big show next door.

ADJACENT TO WATERSIDE THEATRE, on a tract of old-growth forest, are the Elizabethan Gardens, a conceptually imagined formal pleasure garden of Tudor England. Stroll down the paths indicated on the map and turn at the fountain, and here on a pedestal under the leaves of the live oaks stands an idyllic statue of Virginia Dare as a young Indian maiden clad only in a fishnet. Carved from milky Carrara marble in 1859 by Maria Louise Lander, an American expatriate living in Rome, the "Dare Venus" has a history as rich and tempestuous as the big show next door.

Lost in a shipwreck off the coast of Spain in 1860, the statue spent two years at the bottom of the Atlantic before salvage crews raised it and resold it to Lander. Recovered and restored, it crossed the ocean to America, where it was almost lost again, this time to a structure fire. Undamaged by the flames, it was installed in a bay window of the sculptor's home in Washington, D.C. She reportedly greeted it every day with, "You look beautiful this morning, Virginia."

When Lander died in 1926, she willed the statue to the Literary and Historical Society of North Carolina, which displayed the seminude young woman along with portraits of Confederate heroes. The Italian marble Virginia suffered verbal complaints and physical vandalism. In the late 1930s, the space it occupied was converted to an office for a justice of the North Carolina Supreme Court, but within weeks an employee declared the statue embarrassing, and the justice had it removed to the basement. Soon afterward, the statue was shipped to Roanoke Island, where it was housed in a storage shed. In 1946, the shed blew down during a storm, and Virginia Dare went underwater again, although this time her recovery from the shallow sound proved neither as difficult nor as

This statue of Virginia Dare, imagined as a young maiden, is as resilient as the drama that celebrates her birth. Donated by Paul Green to the Garden Club of North Carolina, in 1953 the statue became part of the permanent statuary displayed in the Elizabethan Gardens. Photo by Delena Gray Ostrander

time consuming as her first plunge below the waves. There was talk of breaking the statue down with hammers; it had become a white elephant.

"Good gracious alive," said playwright Paul Green when he heard the rumors. "That would be a sin."

Green accepted legal possession of the statue from the state with "thanks and trepidation," installing what he called the "white-souled creature" by a reflecting pool on his property in Chapel Hill. "I'll shelter her here against breakage as best I can," he wrote. "Although I can't say the same as to the weather."

There she remained until Green presented her to the Garden Club of North Carolina. In 1953, she became part of the permanent statuary displayed in the Elizabethan Gardens. To me, she symbolizes the show: a radiant survivor of fire and flood, forever ageless, forever beautiful.

The cast and crew of *The Lost Colony*'s 80th anniversary season. Photo by Delena Gray Ostrander

The Lost Colony's Eightieth Anniversary Season

ARTISTIC STAFF

Director: Ira David Wood III

Production Designer: William Ivey Long

Lighting Designer: Joshua C. Allen

Music Director: McCrae Hardy

Choreographer/Assistant Director: Pam Atha

Sound Designer: Michael Rasbury

Fight Director: Robert Midgette

Stunt Coordinator: Jason Paul Tate

CAST OF CHARACTERS (*In Order of Appearance*)

Historian: Don Bridge

Uppowoc: Christopher M. Flores

King Wingina: John Bennett

Chief Manteo: Joey Cassella

Manteo's Wife: Betsy Head

Wano: Erlin Zavala

Wanchese: Philip Culton

Captain Arthur Barlowe: Christopher Keil

Captain Philip Amadas: Tucker Ward

Father Martin: Nicholas Baggarley

Tom Harris (Old Tom): Robert Hooghkirk

Landlord: Christopher Charleston

Master of the Queen's Ceremonies:
    Landon Ferrell

Pavane Dancers: Carey Blackburn, Jessica
    Burrell, Megan Daniel, Matt Gabbard,
    Joe Lisi, Wyatt Neff, Jane Kiley Simmons,
    David Thomas Smith

Governor John White: Terry Edwards

Eleanor White (Dare): Henson Milam

Ananias Dare: Daniel Dutot

Ralph Lane: Christopher Charleston

Simon Fernando: Jamil Zraikat

Queen Elizabeth I: Emily Asbury

Page: Kamilah Brooks, Sunday Emery Lane

Sir Walter Raleigh: Daniel Prillaman

John Borden: Ethan Lyvers

Dame Coleman: Pam Atha

John Cage: Phillip Rast

George Howe: Kole McKinley

Joyce Archard: Darian Rutter

Jane Jones: Megan Glover

Alice Chapman: Gabi Stephens

Elizabeth Glane: Megan Daniel

Margaret Lawrence: Mila Bolash

Margery Harvey: Caitlyn Leach

Agona: Patsy Hart

Torch 1: Forrest Harlan

Torch 2: Landon Ferrell

Queen's Messenger: Kelsea Tyler

Burning Girl: Jane Kiley Simmons,
    Darian Rutter

The Sentinel: Calvin Noble

The Runner: Jared Eng-Hong

CHOIR

Mila Bolash, Louisa Britt, Christopher Charleston, Delphon "DJ" Curtis Jr.,
Megan Glover, Gabe Hoyer, Kaleb Jenkins, Bethany K. Johnson, Caitlyn Leach,
Laura Long, Phillip Rast, Gabi Stephens, Tucker Ward

DANCERS

Alexandra Chevrier, Sarah Davis, Zuni Gresham, Darcy Grigg, JoBeth Hardin,
Jake Johnson, Claire Jones, Hank Santos, Galen Schneider, Dillon Smith,
Heidi Waldenmaier, Drew Yowell

ACTOR TECHNICIANS

Carey Blackburn, Jessica Burrell, Megan Daniel, Landon Ferrell, Jared Eng-Hong,
Matt Gabbard, Forrest C. Harlan, Betsy Head, Lennon Hu, Christopher Keil,
Joe Lisi, Caroline May, Vitally Mayes, Austin Mejia, Kole McKinley, Wyatt Neff,
Calvin Noble, Darian Rutter, Jane Kiley Simmons, David Thomas Smith,
Colin Tripp, Kelsea Tyler, Grant VanderVoort, Jonathan Varillas

COLONISTS

Riya Braunstein, Kamilah Ann Ra'Nae Brooks, Wynn Gardner, Ashlynn Hardison,
Matthew Holton, Sunday Emery Lane, Chloe Grace Lias, Jaylen Lindsay,
Hart Moseley, Thomas Shriner, Tenley Simpson

PRODUCTION STAFF

Production Stage Manager: Jennifer Gregory

Technical Director: John Underwood

Associate Music Director: Jordan W. Prescott

Master Electrician: Bri Weintraub

Costume Shop Manager: Charity Sellers

Properties Master: Brandon Cheney

Sound Engineer: Jake Newcomb

Special Effects: Stephen Turner

Associate Production Designer: Brian Mear

Associate Costume Designer: Mariah Hale

Assistant Stage Managers: Sarah Dove,
Dennis Patrick McGinnis IV

Associate Lighting Designer: Noah Trimner

Fight Captain: Philip Culton

Dance Captain: Sarah Davis

Assistant Technical Director: Kyle Hoehn

Assistant Costume Shop Manager:
Jeri Elizabeth Meador

Assistant Master Electrician: Monika Cruson

Props Assistant: Emma Anderson

Assistant Sound Engineer: David Bost
Electrics Crew Chief: Sydney Norris
Follow Spot Operators: Elton Bradley,
   Jesse Byron
Master Carpenter: Kelsy Sedmak

Cutter Draper: Amanda Ferg
Wardrobe Supervisor: Kelsey Musselman
Wardrobe Stitchers: Kieron Cotter, Sydni Hayes,
   Caitie Matheny, Kelsey Marie, Cheyenne
   Wheeler, Anna Zimmerman

ADMINISTRATIVE STAFF

Chief Executive Officer: Bill Coleman
Associate Producer: Lance Culpepper
Director of Advancement: Nancy Figiel
Office Manager: Terry Fowler

Accounting Manager: Terri Lowry-Wingo
Maintenance Supervisor: Crystal Simpson
Ticket Office Manager: Janelle Parrish
Marketing Coordinator: Laurel Anne Darden

THEATER STAFF

Box Office Supervisor: Charles H. Massey
Ticket Specialists: Amy Gross, Cynthia Sellers
House Manager: Jacklyn Pfuhl
Concierge: Logan Marshall

Child Supervisors: Danielle Lane, Jennifer Lias
Ushers: Michelle Hayman, Cameron Parrish,
   John Whitaker

AUTHOR'S ACKNOWLEDGMENTS

*T*his book would not have happened without Barbara Leary. Her firm encouragement and gentle guidance gave me the confidence I needed when I was not sure I could write this story coherently. For her unwavering faith in an untested writer, I am truly grateful.

Many individuals helped: Alice Maniloff put me in touch with Paul Green Jr. Gail Hutchison arranged introductions to *Lost Colony* alumni and loaned me souvenir programs. Lynn Lockrow gave me relevant books, monographs, and pamphlets. I would also like to thank Myles Friedman of Circle City Books in Pittsboro, North Carolina, who procured books for research, and Jim McDiarmid, who read as I wrote and who helped me out of writer's block a couple of months into the project. And I am grateful to editor Stephen Kirk for bringing greater clarity to the story and polishing the final manuscript.

I especially want to thank my darling wife, Elizabeth, who did everything in her power to create extra time for me to research and write. She is my superhero.

For allowing me to move freely around the backstage areas throughout the season, giving me the access I needed to write this book, I want to thank Bill Coleman, producer of *The Lost Colony* and CEO of the Roanoke Island Historical Association, and Lance Culpepper, associate producer.

Which brings me to technical director Johnny Underwood; my presence backstage never would have been accepted by the 2017 company without his blessing. Thanks, dawg.

Most of all, I want to thank the cast and crew of the 2017 *Lost Colony*, who took me in as one of their own. To come back after nearly twenty years and see this show lovingly rendered by capable young hands was thrilling. I hope this book is a testament to their dedication.

—— DWAYNE WALLS JR.

PUBLISHER'S ACKNOWLEDGMENTS

*S*o many people helped to nurture this passion project. In particular, I want to thank Gail Hutchison, for keeping the memories of so many alumni souls in her care and for opening her home to me on my frequent visits to Roanoke Island; Carl Curnutte, the first person I called for an interview, who ended up giving so much more; Mike Campbell, the first to respond with stories; Robert Midgette, for believing in this project from the beginning; Jamie Anderson, owner of Downtown Books, for indulging my questions about the business of book selling; lebame houston, for rummaging through archives for me and remembering stories I had long forgotten; David Miller, for sharing his photo archives; Delena Gray Ostrander, Eden Saunders, Duane Cochran, and Jamil Zraikat, whose photos make the book beautiful; Lance Culpepper, for paving the way; and Ira David Wood III, who gave so generously of his time and insights. I want to thank Ainslie Campbell for her editorial services and for sourcing great stories from alumni; Julie Allred for helping me navigate the unfamiliar aspects of book publishing; and Steve Kirk for his editorial skill and guidance.

I deeply appreciate my author and collaborator Dwayne Walls, whose talent as a storyteller was obvious to me from his first essay. I'm glad we took this leap of faith together!

I am grateful to my daughter-in-law, Christina Sherlock, for her business savvy and for scraping me off the ceiling a time or two, and to my son, Sean Sherlock, who as little "William Wythers" shared *The Lost Colony* experience with me. I am thankful for their good-humored encouragement of my adventures in optimism and for bringing Eleanor, Virginia, and Caroline into the world, making me want to create books about dreams and dreamers.

Finally, I offer a heartfelt thank you to my dear friend and co-conspirator, Elizabeth Evans. Her unwavering support, patience, and wise counsel made the dream of this book possible.

— BARBARA LEARY

KEEPERS OF THE DREAM

We are grateful to the following for so generously supporting the publication of *Backstage at* The Lost Colony.

Wade Barber

John Bennett

Andrea Braymiller

Elly Brown

Johnny Burchett

Marilyn and Chris Chappell

Aaron Cook

Elizabeth Evans and Jon Glass

Ron and Melissa Ferrell

Frank Garciarubio

Susan Campbell Gentry

Eric Green

Monica and Rex Hart

Lynn Hays

Cecelia Fields Hughes

Gail F. Hutchison

George Jack

Laura Brown Lancaster and
    Jamie Evans in memory of
    John Martin Turner

Arturo E. Lara

Julia Angeline LaVault

Karen and Albert Leary

Sara Mackey

Robert Midgette

David Miller

Renee Townsend Mills

Cynthia Ortman

Nicholas C. Parker

Jana D. Peedin in honor of
    John Underwood

Caroline Pendleton-Hillmar

Julie A. Richardson

Larissa Brown Roughton

Christina and Sean Sherlock

Laurel Smylie

John L. Thomas

Ira David Wood III

Zig Zibit

Lauren J. Zimmerman

SELECT BIBLIOGRAPHY

Avery, Laurence G., ed. *A Paul Green Reader*. Chapel Hill: University of North Carolina Press, 1998.

———, ed. *A Southern Life: Letters of Paul Green, 1916-1981*. Chapel Hill: University of North Carolina Press, 1994.

Bell, Albert Q. *Actors in the Colony: 16th Century*. Roanoke Island, NC: Ben Dixon MacNeill, 1946.

Carr, Dawson. *NC 12: Gateway to the Outer Banks*. Chapel Hill: University of North Carolina Press, 2016.

Cliff, Nigel. *The Shakespeare Riots: Revenge, Drama, and Death in Nineteenth-Century America*. New York: Random House, 2007.

Cotton, Sallie Southall. *The White Doe: The Fate of Virginia Dare. An Indian Legend*. Philadelphia: J. B. Lippincott Company, 1901). Facsimile ed., Charleston, SC: Bibliolife, 2017.

Gray, R. Wayne, and Nancy Beach Gray. *Legendary Locals of the Northern Outer Banks*. Charleston, SC: Arcadia Publishing, 2015.

Green, Paul. *Dramatic Heritage*. New York: Samuel French, 1953.

———. *The Lost Colony: An Outdoor Play in Two Acts*. Chapel Hill: University of North Carolina Press, 1937.

———. *The Lost Colony: A Symphonic Drama in Two Acts*. Memorial ed. Chapel Hill: University of North Carolina Press, 1946.

———. *The Lost Colony: A Symphonic Drama of American History*. Roanoke Island ed. Chapel Hill: University of North Carolina Press, 1954.

Harrison, Molly, and Whiting Lee Schindel. *Manteo Walking Tour and the Roanoke Island Guidebook*. Manteo, NC: One Boat Guides, 2006.

Horn, James. *A Kingdom Strange: The Brief and Tragic History of the Lost Colony of Roanoke*. New York: Basic Books, 2010.

Hudson, Marjorie. *Searching for Virginia Dare: A Fool's Errand*. Winston-Salem: Press 53, 2013.

Koch, Frederick H., ed. *American Folk Plays*. New York: D. Appleton-Century Company, Inc., 1939.

———, ed. *Carolina Folk-Plays*. New York: Henry Holt and Company, 1928.

Lost Colony Souvenir Program, The. Manteo, NC: Roanoke Island Historical Association, 1954, 2006, 2017.

McMullan, Philip S., Jr. *Beechland and the Lost Colony*. Nags Head, NC: Pamlico & Albemarle Publishing, 2014.

Powell, William S. *Paradise Preserved: A History of the Roanoke Island Historical Association*. Chapel Hill: University of North Carolina Press, 1965.

Quinn, David Beers. *The Lost Colonists: Their Fortune and Probable Fate*. Raleigh: America's Four Hundredth Anniversary Committee, N.C. Department of Cultural Resources, 1984.

Sadler, Lynn Veach, ed. *Paul Green's Celebration of Man*. Sanford, NC: Human Technology Interface, Ink, 1994.

Saunders, Keith. *The Independent Man: The Story of W. O. Saunders and His Delightfully Different Newspaper*. Washington, DC: Saunders Press, 1962.

Simpson, Bland. *The Great Dismal: A Carolinian's Swamp Memoir*. Chapel Hill: University of North Carolina Press, 1990.

Stick, David. *The Outer Banks of North Carolina, 1584–1958*. Chapel Hill: University of North Carolina Press, 1958.

Sumner, Mark Reese. *A Survey of Outdoor Drama Production Techniques*. New York: American National Theatre and Academy, 1968.

Sumner, Mark Reese, ed. *An Amphitheatre for Epic Drama*. Chapel Hill: University of North Carolina Institute of Outdoor Drama, 1974.

Weir, Alison. *The Life of Elizabeth I*. New York: Ballantine Books, 1998.

Whedbee, Charles Harry. *Legends of the Outer Banks and Tar Heel Tidewater*. Winston-Salem: John F. Blair, 1966.

INDEX OF NAMES

ABOUT THE AUTHOR

Photo by Frederick V. Nielsen II

Son of a journalist and a teacher, DWAYNE WALLS JR. was born and raised in North Carolina. He worked in regional theater throughout the Southeast and spent five seasons with *The Lost Colony* before moving to New York City to build sets and props for television, film, and theater, including NBC's *Saturday Night Live*. Walls is a member in good standing of the International Alliance of Theatrical Stage Employees Local One. He and his wife, Elizabeth, live in Pittsboro, North Carolina.

Photo by Delena Gray Ostrander